Rationale

Reprinted with permission from *Not Strictly by the Numbers*
© Carolina Mathematics/Carolina Biological Supply Company,
Burlington, NC.

As this cartoon suggests, part of the challenge of teaching reading in mathematics
stems from confusion over what "reading mathematics" actually means. Is it being able
to read expressions with mathematical symbols? Is it being able to comprehend printed
numerical data? Or is it being able to comprehend worded passages in, say, a
mathematics textbook?

In this supplement to the manual *Teaching Reading in the Content Areas: If Not Me, Then
Who? (TRCA Teacher's Manual)*, "reading mathematics" means the ability to make sense
of everything that is on a page — whether the page is a worksheet, a spreadsheet, an
overhead transparency, a computer screen, or a page in a textbook or journal — in
other words, any resource that students might use to learn and apply mathematics.

Why should students learn to read mathematics text? Martinez and Martinez (2001) in
Reading and Writing to Learn Mathematics discuss what happens when children read and
write mathematics:

> For starters, their learning incorporates some key ideas in the National Council of
> Teachers of Mathematics new *Principles and Standards for School Mathematics* (NCTM,
> 2000). They learn to use language to focus on and work through problems, to
> communicate ideas coherently and clearly, to organize ideas and structure
> arguments, to extend their thinking and knowledge to encompass other perspectives
> and experiences, to understand their own problem-solving and thinking processes as

well as those of others, and to develop flexibility in representing and interpreting ideas. At the same time, they begin to see mathematics, not as an isolated school subject, but as a life subject — an integral part of the greater world, with connections to concepts and knowledge encountered across the curriculum (see the Process Standards Problem Solving, Reasoning and Proof, Communication, Connections, and Representation). (p. 5)

A second reason students need to learn how to read mathematics is that reading mathematics requires unique knowledge and skills not taught in other content areas. For instance, mathematics students must be able to read not only from left to right, as they do in other subject areas, but also from right to left (as when reading an integer number line), from top to bottom or vice versa (as when reading from tables), and even diagonally (when reading some graphs).

Third, mathematics texts contain more concepts per word, per sentence, and per paragraph than any other kind of text (Brennan & Dunlap, 1985; Culyer, 1988; Thomas, 1988). In addition, these concepts are often abstract, so it is difficult for readers to visualize their meaning.

Fourth, authors of mathematics texts generally write in a very terse or compact style. Each sentence contains a lot of information, and there is little redundancy. Sentences and words often have precise meanings and connect logically to surrounding sentences. Students who want to read mathematics texts quickly — as they might a short story in their language arts class — may miss significant details, explanations, and the underlying logic.

Mathematics also requires students to be proficient at decoding not only words but also numeric and nonnumeric symbols. Consequently, the reader must shift from "sounding out" words such as *plus* or *minus* to instantly recognizing their symbolic counterparts, + and –.

Even the layout of a mathematics text can inhibit comprehension. Students often scan a page of text looking for examples, graphics, or problems to be solved, skipping worded passages filled with crucial information.

Further, many mathematics textbooks are written above the grade level for which they are intended. Therefore, the vocabulary and sentence structure in a mathematics textbook are often especially difficult for the students using these texts.

Finally, publishers of many mathematics textbooks are including longer passages of prose — verbal text — and students and teachers alike need to understand how to navigate these passages successfully. Exhibit 1 illustrates this apparent trend in mathematics texts. Taken from a recently published textbook, *Discovering Algebra: An Investigative Approach* (Murdoch, Kamischke, & Kamischke, 2000), the text on this page (and throughout the book) is markedly different from other, more "traditional" mathematics text pages, which typically contain short verbal passages, a few examples, and a set of problems for students to solve.

Exhibit 1. Lesson on Fractals

Lesson 0.1: The Same yet Smaller

In this lesson you'll review some concepts related to fractional parts. You'll learn to draw a fractal design in the investigation, and then you'll review how to add, subtract, multiply, and divide fractions.

Investigation 0.1.1: Sierpinski Triangle and Fractional Parts

Investigations are a very important part of this course. Often you will discover new concepts in an investigation, so be sure to take an active role.

You can draw some interesting figures that have the characteristic that smaller parts added to the drawing look like the original. The procedures involved are very simple and, if you draw carefully you can create some beautiful designs. This investigation will introduce you to one such figure called the Sierpinski triangle.

You will need a pencil, a straightedge, and the isometric dot paper worksheet for this investigation.

Part 1: Drawing the Sierpinski Triangle

Look at the large triangle labeled Stage 0. In a fractal design, the Stage 0 figure is the starting shape. You'll make the same changes to this figure repeatedly to create the fractal design.

Stage 1 Start with the triangle labeled Stage 1. To create the Stage 1 figure, draw line segments to connect the midpoints of each side of the triangle.

Stage 2 Start with the triangle labeled Stage 2. Connect the midpoints to create the Stage 1 figure again. Next mark the midpoint of each side in each small triangle. Draw line segments to connect the midpoints in the upward-pointing triangles only.

Stage 3 Start with the triangle labeled Stage 3. Re-create the Stage 2 figure in this triangle. Next mark the midpoint of each side in each of the smallest triangles. Draw line segments to connect the midpoints in the upward-pointing triangles only. Check to see that your Stage 3 figure looks like the one at right.

Stage 4 If you want to create a Stage 4 figure, start with the large triangle in the lower half of the worksheet. First connect the midpoints of the large triangle, and continue connecting the midpoints of each smaller upward-pointing triangle at each new stage until you have 81 small upward-pointing triangles.

---
2   Chapter 0: Fractals

Note: From *Discovering Algebra: An Investigative Approach* Preliminary Edition Vol.1 (p. 2), by J. Murdock, E. Kamischke, and E. Kamischke. Copyright 2000 by Key Curriculum Press, 1150 65th Street, Emeryville, CA 94608, 1-800-995-MATH. Reprinted with permission.

No wonder reading mathematics presents such unique challenges. As one experienced educator shares:

> I have reached the conclusion that for my students to reach their potential as mathematicians, they must learn to comprehend mathematical texts, that is, texts constructed of numbers, abstract symbols, and — yes — words. It follows logically from this conclusion, then, that someone — mathematics teachers? — must teach them to do so. (Fuentes, 1998, p. 81)

Other mathematics educators agree. For example, Reehm and Long (1996) write:

> Current recommendations for instruction in mathematics make the need for strategic reading of mathematics texts even more crucial than in the past. . . . There is a place and a need for skill development in reading for the purpose of understanding mathematics concepts. . . . The best place to teach the specific reading skills necessary for mathematics is in the mathematics classroom. . . . (pp. 35–36)

For these reasons — and for others that are explained in this supplement — we have written *Teaching Reading in Mathematics*. In this manual, we explore what literacy in mathematics involves. We also present suggestions and strategies teachers can share with their students to help them become more proficient in reading and communicating in mathematics.

Specifically, we

- examine what the research says about the role of the reader, the role of climate, and the role of text features in mathematics as well as their implications for instruction;

- present math-specific examples of the strategies included in the *TRCA Teacher's Manual* so that mathematics teachers can see how to use and apply these strategies in their classes; and

- present additional strategies to help students become more proficient in reading mathematics.

Section 1
Three Interactive Elements of Reading

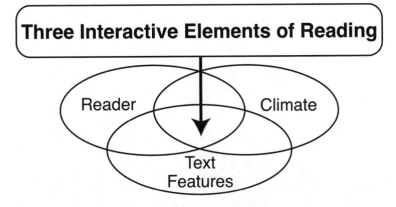

Introduction

As outlined in the second edition of the *TRCA Teacher's Manual*, reading is a constructive process in which readers interact with text, using prior knowledge and experience to make connections, generate hypotheses, and make sense of what they read.

Too often, when students have trouble comprehending a textbook, teachers opt not to use the textbook and to teach mathematics concepts by lecturing about them. These teachers may think they are helping students by translating text material into verbal explanations, diagrams, and charts. However, "when we see these practices in mathematics classrooms, we see instructors in the process of constructing understandings for their students and then handing them over" (Fuentes, 1998, p. 82). In essence, students are deprived of the opportunity to make their own connections and to wrestle with ideas in order to make sense of them.

If students are to construct their own meaning from mathematics text, how can teachers guide and support this process?

Teaching students to comprehend mathematical text entails

- helping students assume their role as readers of mathematics,

- establishing a climate that is conducive to reading and learning mathematics,

- introducing students to the role that text features — vocabulary and text style — play in comprehension, and

- equipping students with strategies to learn new concepts and comprehend mathematics text content.

The Role of the Reader

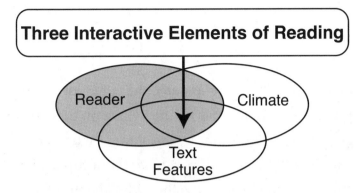

Three Interactive Elements of Reading

Reader · Climate · Text Features

Things to Think About

1. How do students' experiences and prior knowledge of mathematics affect their learning?

2. How can teachers help students develop rich, organized knowledge structures and networks in mathematics?

3. How can teachers motivate students to learn and practice reading strategies?

"Don't tell me why. Just tell me how," the student urged, as the teacher tried to explain the reasoning behind how to solve a mathematics problem the student was working on in study hall. The student didn't want to be bothered by what he considered "extra" input. He was eager to get the answer. Like many readers of mathematics text, he wasn't eager to do the work of constructing meaning. He was more interested in finding a procedure he could use to get the correct answer than in learning how to explain a process or communicate discoveries.

Yet comprehending mathematics, like any other subject, is a constructive process. Research (e.g., Siegel & Borasia, 1992) has shown that "in order to acquire mathematical expertise in a durable and useful form, students need to construct mathematical knowledge and create their own meaning of the mathematics they encounter" (p. 19).

What roadblocks might prevent readers from constructing meaning when reading mathematics text? A number of potential pitfalls in readers' *prior knowledge* and *mental disposition* can create difficulty when reading to learn mathematics.

M☐REL

Prior Knowledge

Two areas that can prevent learning from text are inadequate prior knowledge and prior knowledge that is not organized or accessible in long-term memory.

As discussed in the *TRCA Teacher's Manual*, the extent of learners' prior knowledge and experience has a direct effect on their acquiring new knowledge and skill. For example, the student who does not understand addition will be ill equipped to learn multiplication. Similarly, the student who never learns the "why" behind the "how" of solving certain mathematics problems will have a hard time applying skills used in one type of problem to other types.

This means that students who rely on algorithms alone to solve mathematics problems may find mathematics more difficult as they progress through their school years. Sometimes well-intentioned parents try to help children be more efficient by teaching them algorithms — tried-and-true ways to get answers using procedures like carrying and borrowing. These algorithms, devised as paper-and-pencil procedures, were designed to be quick and efficient. However, they often do not help people understand why they work. In fact, algorithms can make understanding more difficult (see a Mathematics for Parents Newsletter on Place Value (n.d.), Wisconsin Center for Education Research).

However, having a rich background in mathematics is not always a guarantee that a student will be able to solve more complex mathematics problems; the learner's prior knowledge must also be organized and accessible in long-term memory. Alvarez and Risko (cited in Fuentes, 1998) assert that it is this organized body of knowledge that learners access while reading:

> The richer and more organized a reader's knowledge structures and networks are for a given topic, the better he or she will manipulate them in response to the text and the more likely that he or she will achieve appropriate understanding of the topic. (p. 82)

This means that in mathematics class, students must develop organized constructs that help them understand and explain how similar concepts and procedures are related to one another. If they do not, then they will have a difficult time recalling what they have learned and seeing how to apply procedures or concepts in a later chapter or a different context.

For example, one feature of many mathematics texts is that concepts are introduced but not discussed again for several chapters. As Smith and Kepner (1981) explain, mathematics concepts may be "developed in a spiral curriculum in which concepts, words, and symbols are developed and practiced, then followed by a period of disuse" (p. 10). When students merely memorize definitions for these concepts, words, and symbols and then the concepts appear again later in the text, teachers have to spend time re-teaching before beginning the lesson. However, if students develop a thorough and organized knowledge structure and network about this content, they will be able to recall and use that prior knowledge more quickly and effectively.

Instructional Implications

Teachers can use a number of strategies to help students acquire and access rich, well-organized knowledge structures and networks in mathematics.

First, students must recognize the importance of being able to activate and access their prior knowledge. As discussed in the *TRCA Teacher's Manual*, teachers can show students how to activate their prior knowledge of a topic they will be studying by demonstrating basic pre-reading techniques such as

- brainstorming ideas that a topic brings to mind;

- previewing a passage, noting headings and bold print; and

- constructing a graphic organizer, web, or outline from passage headings for use in note taking.

Naturally, teachers also need to ensure that their students have a sufficient prior knowledge base before introducing new material.

Discovering what students already know about a topic helps teachers design instruction around the missing knowledge. A number of strategies can help teachers determine what students know before they begin studying a new topic:

- Semantic Mapping (p. 77)

- Word Sort (p. 86)

- Anticipation/Prediction Guide (p. 95)

- Knowledge Rating Chart (p. 108)

- K-W-L (p. 109)

- Problematic Situation (p. 116)

- Learning Log (p. 132)

Teachers also can help their students learn how to process, organize, and store new information in their long-term memory through the use of graphic organizers (see page 101). Graphic organizers are visual maps or representations that can describe how information in a chapter or a book is organized, or highlight the essential characteristics of a specific concept. Initially, teachers should model for students how to create and use a graphic organizer. For example, teachers may want to provide students with an advance organizer at the beginning of a new unit. Advance organizers include introductory outlines, maps, and webs that help students make connections between what they already know about a topic and what they will be learning. In addition, advance organizers provide students with a visual of the overall structure of key concepts and procedures that will be covered and how these fit together.

The first few advance organizers that a teacher shares with students should be teacher constructed. Eventually, the teacher can leave some spaces in the organizer for students to fill in as the class progresses through the unit. Exhibit 2 is an example of a partially completed advance organizer for a chapter on probability.

Exhibit 2. Advance Organizer for a Text Chapter on Probability

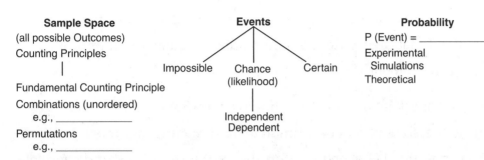

Directions: Save this sheet. Fill in the definitions, diagrams, and examples as we work through Chapter 11. This will be a useful study guide.

Additional types of graphic organizers include semantic and concept maps (see pages 101–105 and 121–122 in this supplement). Again, teachers should model for students how to represent the essential elements of a concept and explain how these are related. Ultimately, students should practice constructing their own meaning of the text content or of a concept by creating their own ways of visually representing the information. And, by sharing a variety of graphic organizers on the same content, students can deepen their understanding of concepts.

In addition to helping students learn how to process, organize, and store new information in their long-term memory, regular use of these kinds of graphic organizers in the classroom can increase comprehension, retention, and recall of information (Jones, Palincsar, Ogle, & Carr, 1987). Moreover, constructing meaning through a visual organizer can challenge students to restructure misconceptions in their existing schema rather than distort new information to fit their beliefs (Fuentes, 1998).

Mental Disposition

Exemplary mathematics educators know that students' attitudes about reading and learning mathematics affect their achievement. Of particular concern, then, are reports that students' motivation to learn wanes over time. For example, Holloway (1999) notes that "intrinsic motivation for literacy and other academic subjects declines in middle school" (p. 80). What can teachers do to increase students' motivation to learn from reading mathematics text?

In addition to connecting reading assignments to students' real-world experiences, teachers need to show students that becoming effective consumers of mathematics text has value. Students need to see firsthand that practicing the right reading strategies will improve their achievement.

This is especially true of struggling readers. Some readers who struggle also have a poor attitude toward reading and often don't see the connection between the effort they put forth to read and complete their assignments and the grades they earn in class. Marzano, Pickering, and Pollock (2001) cite a set of studies demonstrating that simply showing students that added effort improves their achievement actually increases students' achievement. The authors note that since "students might not be aware of the importance of believing in effort," teachers should "explicitly teach and exemplify the connection between effort and achievement" (p. 51).

Instructional Implications

To demonstrate to students how their effort affects their achievement, Marzano et al. (2001) suggest that students periodically assess their level of effort on assignments and track the impact of their effort on the grades they earn. Teachers can give students a set of effort and achievement rubrics (see Exhibit 3 on page 9), which students can use to assess and track their effort and achievement on a chart (see Exhibit 4 on page 10).

When students observe the impact that their effort and attitude have on their progress, they begin to see the value of applying reading strategies to improve their comprehension and learning. They also gain a sense of control over their learning — a crucial step in assuming more responsibility for their own learning.

Exhibit 3. Effort and Achievement Rubrics

Effort and Achievement Rubrics for Mathematics

Scale: 4 = excellent; 3 = good;
2 = needs improvement; 1 = unacceptable

Effort Rubric

4   I worked on my mathematics assignment until it was completed. I pushed myself to continue working on the task even when difficulties arose, when a solution was not immediately evident, or when I had trouble understanding what an author was saying. I used obstacles that arose as opportunities to strengthen my understanding and skills beyond the minimum required to complete the assignment.

3   I worked on my mathematics assignment until it was completed. I pushed myself to continue working on the task even when difficulties arose, when a solution was not immediately apparent, or when I had trouble understanding what an author was saying.

2   I put some effort into my mathematics assignment, but I stopped working when difficulties arose, when a solution was not immediately evident, or when I had trouble understanding what an author was saying.

1   I put very little effort into my mathematics assignment.

Achievement Rubric

4   I exceeded the objectives of the assignment.

3   I met the objectives of the assignment.

2   I met a few of the objectives of the assignment, but didn't meet others.

1   I did not meet the objectives of the assignment.

Notes

Exhibit 4. Effort and Achievement Chart

Student Greg Starek	Assignment	Effort Rubric	Achievement Rubric
Monday, Sept. 21	Read the introduction to proportional reasoning. Conduct an investigation on body measurements: Record measurements in a table that includes ratios of certain measurements, make box plots of data from females and males in the class, and write a paragraph that compares the graphs.	4	4
Wed., Sept. 23	Homework: Complete a problem set involving various ratios in several given data sets.	3	4
Thurs., Sept. 24	Read about proportions, and conduct an investigation solving for an unknown in a proportion. Write an explanation of the process used in the investigation.	3	3
Friday, Sept. 25	Homework: Complete a problem set on writing proportions and solving for an unknown quantity. Read about percents, and conduct an investigation on visualizing and computing percents.	4	4

10

The Role of Climate

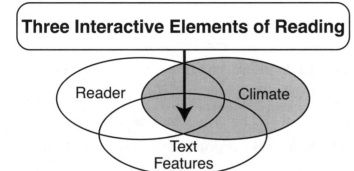

Three Interactive Elements of Reading

Reader   Climate

Text
Features

Things to Think About

1. What does "climate" in the mathematics classroom include?

2. What can mathematics teachers do to create a classroom climate that supports learning?

The National Council of Teachers of Mathematics (2000) has articulated the important role that classroom climate plays in learning:

> More than just a physical setting with desks, bulletin boards, and posters, the classroom environment communicates subtle messages about what is valued in learning and doing mathematics. Are students' discussion and collaboration encouraged? Are students expected to justify their thinking? If students are to learn to make conjectures, experiment with various approaches to solving problems, construct mathematical arguments and respond to others' arguments, then creating an environment that fosters these kinds of activities is essential. (p. 18)

Learning is most likely to occur when students see value in what they are doing, when they believe they can be successful, and when they feel safe. Unfortunately, some students do not see any value in learning mathematics. This is especially true for students who have a history of failure and experiences in which they were criticized or humiliated for taking risks. Perhaps this is a consequence of past mathematics instruction that focused mainly on product rather than on the process of doing mathematics.

We now know that mathematics education should emphasize active, flexible, and resourceful problem solving and should place greater emphasis on the affective dimensions of learning mathematics (National Research Council, 1989, 1990; NCTM, 1989, 1991, 2000). No longer should instruction focus on imitating and memorizing what is presented by the teacher, but rather on "students' problem-solving strategies, including their ability to generate and define problems, as well as their mathematical reasoning and communication" (Siegel & Borasia, 1992, p. 19).

Instructional Implications

In addition to those suggestions given in the *TRCA Teacher's Manual*, there are a number of things mathematics teachers can do to establish a classroom climate that supports learning. First, teachers should shift instruction to emphasize process. Point out to students that there may be more than one way to solve a problem or that, in some situations, there may be multiple solutions. Model for students how you reach a solution, but also let students discuss in groups the steps that they went through to reach their solutions. Another technique is to ask questions that allow for more than one response. For example, you might set up a word problem in which students are told that they have a certain amount of money to spend for camping supplies. Provide a list of items with prices marked, and allow students to "shop" so that they purchase what they think they will need for this scenario, spending an amount that uses their funds yet is within their budget. You might then ask students to write an explanation of their purchases and their calculations.

Another method of easing learners' fears of making mistakes is to give students credit for the effort they put into solving a problem. Certainly, students are being asked to "show" or "explain" their work in class assignments and on assessments. Offer students credit for writing out their thought processes, so that they begin to value process too.

The Role of Text Features

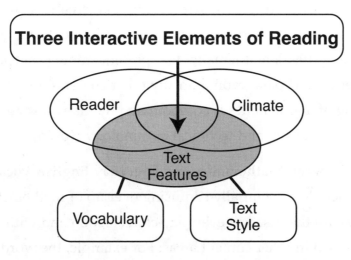

Text features are those aspects of text content and presentation that influence comprehension. In this section, we focus first on vocabulary and then on text style.

Text Features: Vocabulary

Things to Think About

1. Why do students have difficulty learning mathematics vocabulary?

2. What are the best ways to develop students' understanding of mathematics terminology?

There are many reasons that the language and vocabulary used in mathematics can challenge even able readers. In this section we explore four of these and then offer suggestions for addressing each:

1. Conceptual density of mathematics text

2. Complex overlap between mathematics vocabulary and the vocabulary used in "ordinary" English

3. Varied use and large number of mathematics symbols and graphics

4. Need to understand concepts embedded within others concepts

1. Conceptual Density of Mathematics Text

One reason students struggle when reading mathematics is the sheer number of concepts packed into the text. According to Schell (see Reehm & Long, 1996), mathematics text presents more concepts per word, sentence, and paragraph than any other content-area text. "The reading of mathematics is compounded by many abstractions, specialized symbolism, and technical terminology" (p. 36).

2. Overlap Between Mathematics and Everyday English Vocabulary

Moreover, there is a potentially confusing overlap of mathematics vocabulary with that used in everyday conversation and with vocabulary used in other content areas. For example, the word *difference* could easily confuse the young student faced with the question, "What is the difference between 4 and 7?" The student might answer, "Four is even, but seven is odd," when the intended correct response is "three." Even the word *odd* means something different in language arts! And the student who has just arrived in mathematics class from social studies where the class discussed the "radical left" or the student coming from health class where they learned about "free radicals" may be very confused when asked to comprehend the word *radical* in a mathematics text.

There are also terms that in mathematics have a more specialized meaning than they do in everyday English. The words *average* and *similar* are two examples. In Exhibit 5, the first two shapes look similar as that term is used in ordinary English. However, the mathematical meaning of *similar* is more specialized: In order for polygons to be similar, they must have corresponding angles that are equal.

Exhibit 5. Polygons

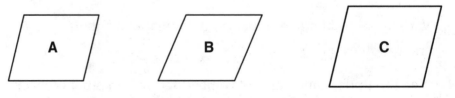

A and C are similar, whereas A and B are not.

3. Use and Number of Mathematics Symbols and Graphics

A third challenge in reading mathematics is that the reader must decode and comprehend not only words but also mathematics signs, symbols, and graphics. This means that students must switch between the skills they use to decode words and the skills needed to decode signs and symbols. Decoding words entails connecting sounds to the alphabetic symbols, or letters. Hence, we say "sound it out" when students have trouble decoding an unfamiliar word. In contrast, mathematics signs and symbols may be pictorial, such as an arrow, or they may refer to an operation (e.g., $\div$) or an expression (e.g., $\geq$). Consequently, students need to learn the meaning of each symbol much like they learn sight words in the English language. In addition, they need to connect each symbol, the idea it represents, and the written or spoken term that corresponds to that idea.

Reading mathematics words and symbols can be especially difficult for struggling readers. Fuentes (1998) explains that "because mathematics writing is unique with its combination of words and symbols and compact style, children not reading at grade level, or children whose primary language is not English, are often at a disadvantage" (pp. 81–82).

Moving between alphabetic symbols and mathematics symbols is made more difficult because of the sheer number of different mathematics symbols used. Reehm and Long (1996) cite a study of textbooks used in grades 4 through 12 which identified 153 of these mathematics symbols. Reehm and Long note that "one hundred thirty of these were found to be common in the five most widely adopted textbook series for seventh and eighth grade mathematics" (p. 36).

To complicate matters, mathematics symbols can have more than one meaning. For example, the symbols **12 $\div$ 4** could represent the concept of sharing ("twelve divided into four equal parts") or could represent grouping ("How many groups of four in twelve?").

Moreover, the same idea and the same translation or wording of the idea can be represented by different symbols:

$$12 \div 4, \quad \frac{12}{4}, \quad 4\overline{)12}$$

Division, therefore, can be conveyed in a variety of ways, and the student must understand that the meaning is the same.

Shuard and Rothery (1984) assert:

> A child needs eventually to understand that there are two ideas (grouping and sharing) and several sets of symbols attached to the word *division*, including the notation $\frac{12}{4}$ which makes the link between division and fractions explicit. A child has a fully operational concept only when all these ideas are seen as aspects of the concept of division, rather than as isolated ideas and notations. (p. 38)

Similarly, the same multiplication fact can be expressed in words: *multiply three by five*; or *three times five*; or *the product of three and five* and in symbols: **3 × 5** or **3(5)** or **3 • 5**.

Shuard and Rothery note that symbols rarely appear alone and can be combined in a variety of ways to communicate different meanings. Thus, the position and order of symbols convey specific meaning. However, irregularities in the rules for combining symbols can cause confusion for some students. Just when students have learned how to decode **3x** in algebra as "3 multiplied by x," they move into calculus, where they must grasp the idea that **δx** does not mean "δ multiplied by x," but rather "an increment in x."

Smith and Kepner (1981) also discuss how this irregularity affects mathematics students as they progress through their studies:

> Initially, "–" represents the binary operation in subtraction; i.e., 5 – 3 means 5 subtract 3. With the introduction of integers, –7 represents a particular seven, namely "negative 7." In this context, the horizontal bar describes which 7 is being considered. Finally, –x refers to the "opposite of x" or the "additive inverse of x." Here –x identifies the monary operation, i.e., an operation of a single number. If students are confused about the exact meaning of a word, symbol, or number, the solution to a sentence like "What is the value of –x when x = –7?" becomes an exercise in frustration. (p. 9)

Children sometimes struggle with where to start to read a combination of symbols. When reading their social studies or language arts textbook, they read from left to right and from the top of the page to the bottom. But when they open their mathematics books, this convention doesn't always apply. For instance, both of the combinations $27 \div 3$ and $3\overline{)27}$ convey the same idea, but the order of the symbols is reversed. Consequently, it is not unusual for young mathematics students to mistakenly conclude that in all division, "the larger number is the one you divide by the smaller number."

Other symbolic representations that students must learn how to interpret are diagrams, graphs, and tables. The ideas expressed in these forms often cannot be expressed as easily in words. Again, students reading mathematics must shift from using skills needed to decode and comprehend prose text on the page to those needed to comprehend the ideas represented in tabular or graphic form. Teachers need to take time to ensure that students can read and interpret these symbolic forms.

4. Need to Understand Embedded Concepts

A fourth reason learning mathematics vocabulary presents unique challenges is the fact that certain concepts in mathematics are defined and understood only as they are embedded within other concepts. Exhibit 6 illustrates this point.

Exhibit 6. Number Systems

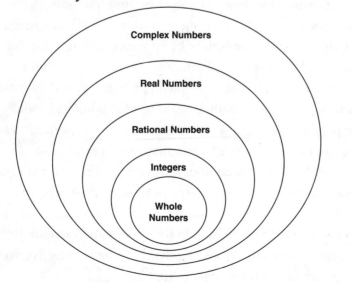

Notes

As Exhibit 6 indicates, the concept of integers is best understood in relation to the concepts of whole numbers and rational numbers. That is, to understand the concept of integers fully, students need to comprehend how this concept fits into a larger scheme that includes other related concepts. Similarly, the concept of rational numbers is understood in relation to the concept of integers. Thus, a natural prerequisite to operating with rational numbers is to work with integers. Real numbers are understood in relation to rational numbers, and so on. In such instances where the understanding of one concept depends upon an understanding of how it is embedded within other known concepts, mathematics teachers need to present vocabulary development activities that delineate the relational nature of concepts.

Instructional Implications

How should teachers address the conceptual density in mathematics text and the confusion that students may experience in interpreting the meaning of language in mathematics text? Teachers might be tempted to use informal terminology in place of the more formal mathematics terminology used in text. They also may be tempted to eliminate the use of mathematics text except for the examples and exercises they contain. Neither of these choices supports the development of literacy in mathematics. NCTM proposes some guidelines that teachers might use when making decisions about terminology use. In *Principles and Standards for School Mathematics*, NCTM (2000) suggests:

> As students articulate their mathematical understanding in the lower grades, they begin by using everyday, familiar language. This provides a base on which to build a connection to formal mathematical language. . . . Beginning in the middle grades, students should understand the role of mathematical definitions and should use them in mathematical work. Doing so should become pervasive in high school. However, it is important to avoid a premature rush to impose formal mathematical language; students need to develop an appreciation of the need for precise definitions and for the communicative power of conventional mathematical terms by first communicating in their own words. Allowing students to grapple with their ideas and develop their own informal means of expressing them can be an effective way to foster engagement and ownership. (p. 63)

How can teachers help students develop a "sight word" level of familiarity with the numerous symbols used in their mathematics text? As with any vocabulary instruction, teachers need to offer students adequate explanations of these symbols and the chance to practice recognizing and using these symbols on a recurring basis. Flash cards are one tool students can use when learning new symbols. Teachers can build in opportunities during class time for students to review these symbols in fun activities, such as Cue Cards (see page 91). In this game, the teacher states a verbal cue for an expression using symbols, and students have to locate the expression on a card. The point is to give students numerous and regular opportunities to review symbols.

Students should also be given opportunities to practice reading and then constructing and analyzing graphs and charts. Many newspapers include bar graphs and pie charts; these "real-life" graphics are ideal for students to practice interpreting data.

A caution specific to mathematics is that students may confuse illustrations with definitions, especially if a common picture is used almost exclusively. Although nonlinguistic representations are helpful in developing recall, teachers should avoid using the same illustration each time they refer to a term. For example, a teacher should picture:

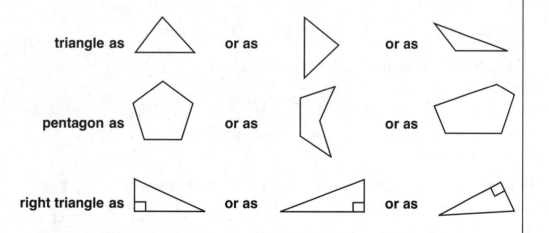

Otherwise, a student may view only the first example as illustrative of the shape.

Teachers can help students grasp embedded concepts as well as how other concepts are related by demonstrating these relationships with graphic organizers. Monroe and Pendergrass (1997) recommend that teachers "teach to the brain's natural capacity for thinking and organizing information" (p. 3). Vocabulary maps, webs, and other types of graphic organizers allow learners to manipulate new ideas, to see how these ideas are related to what they already know, and to integrate their new learning into existing schema or revise that schema to reflect new understanding.

Monroe (1997) recommends that teachers allow students to construct their own graphic organizers, in addition to using those that are teacher constructed. She cites research demonstrating that letting students construct their own organizers may be even more beneficial than asking them to fill in those constructed by their teachers, because students are actively engaged in the construction of meaning when they must process ideas themselves. She also points out that student-constructed graphic organizers are a good barometer of learners' understanding and, as such, are helpful tools for teachers as they plan additional instruction.

Exhibits 7 and 8 are two graphic organizers representing the relationships that exist among mathematics concepts.

Exhibit 7. Semantic Map for Plane Figures

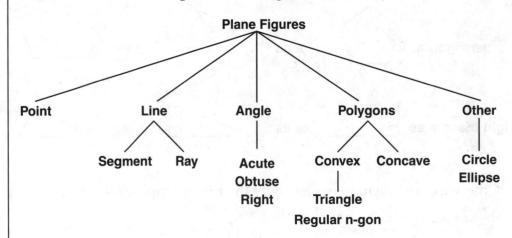

Exhibit 8. Graphic Organizer for Number Systems

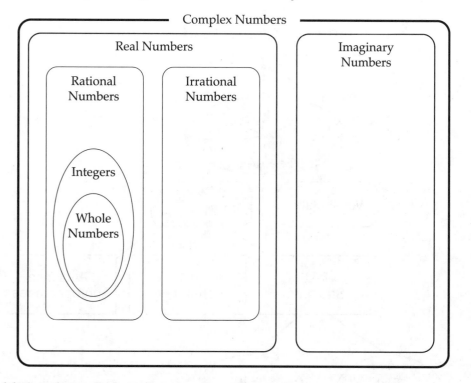

Additional vocabulary development strategies are explained on pages 62–94 of this supplement.

In conclusion, we cannot emphasize too strongly the importance of including vocabulary development work within regular classroom mathematics instruction. Numerous studies (see those cited in Earp, 1970; Earp & Tanner, 1980; and Helwig, Rozek-Tedesco, Tindal, Heath, & Almond, 1999) reveal that a knowledge of mathematics vocabulary directly affects achievement in arithmetic, particularly problem solving. For example, Earp (1970) notes, "Reading comprehension and arithmetic achievement tend to be positively related. Almost without exception instruction in vocabulary and/or reading skills in arithmetic paid off in terms of greater achievement, especially in the area of problem solving" (p. 531).

In addition, Marzano et al. (2001) assert that direct instruction on words that are an integral part of new content has a dramatic impact on learning: "The research by Stahl and Fairbanks (1986) indicates that student achievement will increase by 33 percentile points when vocabulary instruction focuses on specific words that are important to what students are learning" (p. 127).

Text Features: Text Style

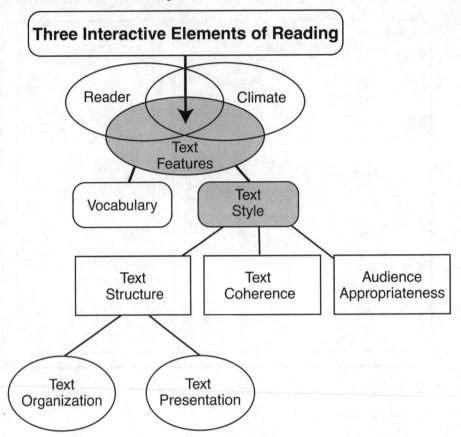

As discussed, comprehending mathematics text depends on the interaction among three key elements: the reader, the climate, and text features. Text features that affect students' comprehension of mathematics text — both positively and negatively — are numerous. The previous section examined one feature of mathematics text, vocabulary, and explained how teachers can plan for and incorporate vocabulary development activities into content instruction.

This section explores text style, more specifically, *text structure*, *text coherence*, and *audience appropriateness*. The first edition of the *TRCA Teacher's Manual* included a discussion of text structure. Since the publication of that manual, however, research and experience have shown that additional characteristics of text style have a significant impact on students' comprehension of textbooks and on teachers' selection of texts. Thus, we have expanded our vision of content-area reading instruction to include these additional components.

Things to Think About

1. What features of mathematics text make reading this text difficult for most students?

2. What responsibility do mathematics teachers have to teach students how to contend with text features such as organization and presentation?

3. What do mathematics teachers need to know about text coherence and audience appropriateness so that they can select reading material that students can understand?

Text Structure

Two aspects of text structure — organization and presentation — have a direct impact on reading comprehension. Therefore, teaching students how to recognize and use text organization and text presentation to aid comprehension can improve student learning. According to Jones et al. (1987), students who are skilled at working with text organization are better able to

- locate key information,

- identify what is important and unimportant,

- synthesize information that appears in different locations within a text or from a number of texts,

- connect new information with what is known, and

- restructure schema to account for new learning.

Similarly, students who are skilled at working with text presentation — how textbook publishers lay out content — comprehend more of what they read. In their synthesis of research on text organization and presentation and the relationship of these text features to students' reading comprehension, Dickson, Simmons, and Kameenui (1995) found the following:

- Well-presented physical text (i.e., text that is visually laid out in a way that makes the organization of the content evident) assists in reading comprehension.

- Text structure and students' awareness of text structure are highly related to reading comprehension.

- Explicit instruction in the physical presentation of text and/or text structure aids in reading comprehension.

Text Organization

Readence, Bean, and Baldwin (2001) use the term *macrostructure* to describe a text's overall organizational pattern. Macrostructure is the "the larger ideational framework that binds together its complex system of paragraphs" (p. 48). Organizational patterns such as cause-effect, description, and comparison-contrast are examples of macrostructures.

Authors of mathematics text typically do not use the same macrostructures to organize their ideas that authors of other content-area texts use. Therefore, the organizational patterns discussed in the *TRCA Teacher's Manual* — the macrostructures readers typically encounter in expository text — are not common to mathematics text.

Why don't authors of mathematics text organize their material in the manner used by authors of other kinds of text? Answers to this question vary. Lindquist (1987) asserts that the organization of mathematics text is unique to this discipline:

> The basic premise that learning is organizing knowledge certainly is true in mathematics. . . . However, we must be cautious in thinking that this organization is parallel to that in other disciplines. To try to impose generic organizational patterns upon a discipline already structured would be counterproductive. (pp. 118–119)

Despite Lindquist's reluctance to impose commonly used text patterns on mathematics text, it is important for mathematics teachers to analyze the textbooks they use to determine what kind of macrostructure is used. Teachers can identify how the material is organized by creating a map or by outlining sample chapters. They might begin by using the text's table of contents as a guide for the outline or map. If the text is well written, the information presented within each unit or chapter or module should follow a consistent pattern. An example of how one textbook presented an outline for a thematic module appears in Exhibit 9.

Exhibit 9. Search and Rescue Module

MODULE 2

SECTION OVERVIEW

1 Looking at Angles

As you learn a rescue skill:
- Name and measure angles
- Classify angles
- Use supplementary and complimentary angles

2 Integers and Coordinates

As you study elevation:
- Compare integers
- Find opposites and absolute values of integers
- Identify and plot points in a coordinate plane

3 Integer Addition and Subtraction

As you explore wind-chill temperatures:
- Use a model to work with integers
- Add and subtract integers

4 Function Models

As you compare rescue options:
- Model a function with a table, an equation, or a graph
- Evaluate expressions with variables

5 Addition and Subtraction Equations

As you explore backpack weights:
- Write addition and subtraction equations
- Solve equations using models and inverse operations

Note: From *Math Thematics* Book 2 (p. 75) by R. Billstein and J. Williamson, 1999, Evanston, IL: McDougal Littel. Copyright 1999 by McDougal Littel Inc. All rights reserved. Reprinted by permission of McDougal Littel Inc.

After determining how the content is organized and creating an outline, map, or other type of structured overview that describes the organization, teachers could give students copies of this representation before students read the text, so that they can see how the material is organized and use this awareness of the text's macrostructure to organize their own thinking and learning when reading.

Other authors have identified certain text types and writing patterns that are found in mathematics text. For example, Shuard and Rothery (1984) discuss five "types" of writing that they assert are commonly found in mathematics text: exposition, instructions, exercises and examples, peripheral writing, and signals. Because these types of writing are parts of the larger text and appear in various places in a mathematics text, they would not be classified as macrostructures. Nevertheless, recognizing and understanding each type of writing may enhance comprehension. Therefore, each of these types is explained below with suggestions for instruction.

Exposition is the explaining of concepts and methods, vocabulary, notation, and rules. The reader is meant to comprehend this material, but not necessarily use this knowledge right away. At times, vocabulary terms are introduced and defined through exposition:

> In reading mathematical exposition, the reader often needs to work out steps in the argument for himself, so it is essential for him to use pencil and paper as he reads, rather than passively reading the text as he would a novel. In text for children, some exposition is not distinguished from exercises — indeed, exposition is often presented as exercises in order to force the reader into an active mode of reading. (Shuard & Rothery, 1984, p. 11)

Instructions, according to Shuard and Rothery, tell the reader to perform a task, such as to draw, complete, or solve. Although text instructions may seem straightforward to the teacher, students can make mistakes when unfamiliar words are used to identify a process or operation. It's a good idea to familiarize students with different ways that instructions are given in a new text. For instance, some authors use the phrase "solve the following . . . ," while others use "complete . . . ," or "find the . . . ," or "evaluate . . . ." To the experienced teacher or student, such varied instructions are clearly synonymous; however, to students whose prior knowledge is limited, a change in instructions can be confusing.

Exercises and **examples** can involve computations, simple problems, or more complex problems. In any case, an exercise may require students to practice the idea just as it is introduced or to apply their knowledge and extend their understanding of the idea presented. It is helpful to point out to students which skills they will need to use in completing the exercises or reading the examples.

Peripheral writing includes introductory remarks, clues, and observations or remarks that help the reader move through the text but are not crucial to understanding or learning. For example, at the beginning of a chapter, the author may remind students, "In the last chapter we learned how to add and subtract fractions. In this chapter, we will learn how to multiply and divide fractions." This introduction helps activate students' prior knowledge and also links that knowledge to the new information students can expect to learn in the chapter.

Sometimes authors include rhetorical questions in the text. For example, after an expository section on polygons, the author may write, "Can you think of other shapes that would fit into this category?" Inexperienced students may find this confusing. Are they supposed to reply to this question in an active way by taking out paper and pencil and making a list of other shapes that could be in the category under discussion? Or is the author simply asking the reader to think about this subject? Since students often are expected to answer questions in their mathematics text, they may find the purpose of these rhetorical questions unclear.

Signals are reader aids that help guide the reader through the page, such as headings and subheadings, bullets, arrows, and the like. Although we discuss signals in an upcoming section on text presentation, we agree with Shuard and Rothery about the important role these features play in the comprehension of mathematics text. Teachers should introduce students early in the school year to the unique signals used by their textbook's publisher. Each publisher selects certain fonts, graphic symbols, and text boxes to signal specific kinds of information. These graphic aids also indicate relationships among ideas and their superordination and subordination. All of these devices help readers navigate through text that at first glance may appear to be disorganized and jumbled. Students need to learn how their text uses typographical signals so that they can become more expert readers.

Roe, Stoodt, and Burns (1995) also have identified types of writing that occur frequently in mathematics. They call these types of writing "writing patterns." Again, these patterns are used to organize pieces of text rather than an entire textbook. Therefore, they would not be classified as macrostructures but, rather, as recurring patterns within the greater macrostructure of the text. As noted about text types described earlier, teachers can use their awareness of these patterns when creating structured overviews for students to use when reading chapters that contain these patterns.

Specifically, the two patterns Roe et al. discuss are the demonstration pattern and the problem pattern. "The demonstration pattern is used to show students the development of processes and concepts" (p. 427). Usually accompanied by an example illustrating the written text, this pattern explicates for students how to work problems. Roe et al. outline three strategies that students can use when reading text written in the demonstration pattern:

1. As they read, students should attempt to work through the example given in the text to determine whether they understand the process. If they reach a different answer than that given in the text, students should work through the example again more slowly, rereading each step to identify where in the process they made an error.

2. Students should try to paraphrase the process in their own words.

3. Students should apply the process they learned to other situations.

Exhibit 10 is an example of the demonstration pattern.

Exhibit 10. Mathematics Text Example of Demonstration Pattern

THE DENSITY PROPERTY

You have already learned that the Density Property works with fractions—between any two fractions there is at least one other fraction. Does the Density Property work for any two rational numbers, such as 1.375 and 1.376?

Example Find some rational numbers between 1.375 and 1.376.

You can use this number line to find numbers between 1.375 and 1.376. Remember that 1.375 = 1.3750 and 1.376 = 1.3760.

```
         1.3751   1.3753   1.3755   1.3757   1.3759
    ◄────┼───┼───┼───┼───┼───┼───┼───┼───┼───┼───┼────►
       1.3750   1.3752   1.3754   1.3756   1.3758   1.3760
```

So, between 1.375 and 1.376 are the rational numbers 1.3751, 1.3752, 1.3753, and so on.

- Are there any rational numbers between 1.3751 and 1.3752? Support your answer.

More Examples Find a rational number between the two numbers of each pair.

A. $^{-}\frac{7}{8}$ and $^{-}0.75$

Write $^{-}\frac{7}{8}$ as $^{-}0.875$ and $^{-}0.75$ as $^{-}0.750$.

Possible answers:
$^{-}0.763, ^{-}0.800, ^{-}0.825$

B. $\frac{3}{5}$ and $\frac{2}{3}$

Write both fractions with a common denominator.

$\frac{3}{5} = \frac{18}{30}$ and $\frac{2}{3} = \frac{20}{30}$.

$\frac{19}{30}$ is between $\frac{3}{5}$ and $\frac{2}{3}$.

Note that many other answers are possible for Examples A and B.

Note: From *Mathematics Plus* (p. 338), by G. M. Burton, M. H. Hopkins, H. C. Johnson, J. D. Kaplan, L. Kennedy, and K. A. Schultz, 1994, Orlando, FL: Harcourt Brace & Company. Copyright 1994 by Harcourt, Inc. Reprinted by permission of the publisher.

The second writing pattern that Roe et al. (1995) identify is the problem pattern. They observe:

> Many readers have significant difficulties reading and understanding word problems, which are mathematical situations that are stated in words and symbols. Even when they can read the words and sentences with facility, many students have difficulty choosing the correct process (operation) to solve the problem. (p. 424)

Often, arithmetic story problems are not organized in a manner that is familiar to young students. Instead, facts and details often appear at the beginning of the problem and the thesis or topic sentence appears at the end (Reutzel, 1983). Consequently, students are not sure what their purpose for reading is until the end of the problem. They may forget or simply not attend to important details of the problem before they find the thesis or topic sentence. As students reach the intermediate and upper grades, more distractors or irrelevant details are included in word problems, which can be further cause for confusion. An added challenge in comprehending and solving story problems is determining the precise meaning of the topic sentence — that is, the question asked or the problem posed.

Teachers need to model for students how to read and analyze word problems. One way to model this process is to use the Think- Aloud strategy (see page 126 in this supplement). As teachers read aloud a particular word problem, they can demonstrate how they go about identifying what the problem is asking, which details are important and which are irrelevant, and which process or operation will help them reach the solution.

Kresse (1984) asserts that modeling effective metacognitive behaviors during problem solving, and then offering students practice in these behaviors, are essential if students are to become independent learners. She recommends explaining to students that the information they need to solve a problem lies in the wording of the problem. Therefore, students should learn how to look for keys for retrieving that information.

Kresse offers a two-part strategy. The first part involves teachers analyzing and preparing for the problem-solving task. Kresse points out that mathematics teachers often explain how a problem is solved, but rarely explain "how they know how." Through their own extensive practice in solving word problems, teachers have formed subconscious generalizations about problem-solving techniques.

Therefore, Kresse contends, teachers should spend time reflecting on and analyzing the keys to process comprehension:

> First, ask yourself how you know the correct process. Try to select just the words necessary to work the problem, to be sure of the correct process. After you select the process words, use a mental cloze procedure[†]. Read the problem with only the words you've chosen. Can you still perform the correct operation? What else can you delete and still work the problem correctly? (p. 599)

After the teacher has modeled his or her metacognitive process, Kresse recommends giving students instruction in these behaviors through a technique she calls the S-Q-R-R strategy:

- **S**urvey the problem. Read the question sentence first.

- **Q**uestion yourself. "What is this asking me to find?" (This provides a purpose for reading the problem word by word.)

- **R**ead the problem aloud in its entirety, and explain how you determine which information is key and which information is extraneous. If appropriate, draw a sketch and label it using the key information.

- Ask, "What is the correct process to solve this problem?"

- Work the problem.

- Check your **R**easoning. Ask, "What process did I use? Why did I choose that process? Was my reasoning correct?"

Roe et al. (1995) suggest another approach to reading verbal problems which they adapted from Earle (1976):

> In this technique, the teacher uses a series of steps to guide students through the written language of the problem. . . .
>
> 1. Read the problem quickly to obtain a general understanding of it. Visualize the problem. Do not be concerned with the numbers.

[†] The cloze procedure deletes some words from a text and replaces them with blanks. The reader must supply the missing words.

2. Examine the problem again. Identify the question you are asked to answer. This question usually comes at the end of the problem, but it may occur anywhere in the problem.

3. Read the problem again to identify the information given.

4. Analyze the problem to see how the information is related. Identify any missing information and any unnecessary information.

5. Compute the answer.

6. Examine your answer. Label the parts of the solution to correspond with the question that the problem asks you to solve. Is your answer sensible? (pp. 425–427)

Although research indicates that teachers define and implement problem-solving instruction in a variety of ways, mathematics educators, textbooks, and classroom resource materials typically rely on a view of problem solving based on Polya's four-step process for problem solving (see Polya, 1957, and Gay, 1999):

1. Understand the problem. Here, students determine the data given, the unknown, the information needed or not needed, and the condition or context of the problem. It may be helpful to draw a sketch including the known information.

2. Devise a plan. This may be as simple as selecting the correct operation demanded by the problem. In more challenging instances, students may need to examine ways in which this problem is similar to others they have solved successfully in the past. If an immediate connection cannot be found, they may need to consider the problem from a different perspective. That is, they may need to find a related problem — one more general but having similar features — and examine how solving that sort of problem can give them hints about how they might attack this problem. They also might restate the problem to make sure that they understand terminology, to ensure that they have understood the whole situation, and to take into account all

essential components involved in the problem. Eventually, they should settle on a plan to come up with a reasonable solution to the problem.

3. Carry out the plan, checking (or proving) that each step is correct.

4. Examine the solution obtained. Check the result to make sure that it is reasonable or solves the problem.

Several additional strategies for working on word problems are offered in this supplement:

- Five-Step Problem Solving (p. 98)

- K-N-W-S (K-W-L for word problems) (p. 112)

- SQRQCQ (p. 125)

- Three-Level Guide (p. 128)

- Word Problem Roulette (p. 130)

Text Presentation

Text presentation refers to (1) the way written material is physically laid out; (2) its visual textual cues, such as headings, captions, bold print, italics, and font size and color; and (3) its illustrations and graphics. These features can either help or hinder comprehension. As discussed in the section on vocabulary, a page of mathematics text may also contain a variety of mathematics symbols and graphics. One page of text might therefore feature short verbal passages, examples containing numeric and nonnumeric symbols, diagrams, graphs, and even photographs.

Teachers need to examine potential textbooks to make sure that the layout of the information on the page clearly supports the development of the content and is not too "busy" or distracting for students to read easily.

A suggestion for helping students work with text presentation is to walk students through their textbook's layout at the beginning of the school year. Point out for students how color and size of font are used to help readers identify sections and subsections within chapters of text. Examine how the publisher of the text uses white space to indicate a change of subject, and point this out to students. Explain that publishers try to incorporate visual cues to help readers locate important ideas. (The *TRCA Teacher's Manual* refers to these as "reader aids.") Model for students how to use headings and font size or color to predict what a section of text will be about.

Text Coherence

Text coherence refers to the degree to which the author's ideas are logically ordered and clearly explained. Effective writers sequence their ideas in a logical manner and clearly demonstrate the relationships among the ideas. Clearly, text coherence is closely related to text organization.

Armbruster (1996) cites numerous studies about the influence that coherence has on reading comprehension. These studies found that comprehension is adversely affected when the main idea is not clearly stated, when the relationships among events are implied rather than explicit, and when irrelevant details are included. Armbruster calls this kind of text "inconsiderate." In contrast, she explains:

> In considerate texts, main ideas are explicitly stated. Explicit main ideas appear in prominent places such as introductions and summaries, headings, and topic sentences at the beginning of sections and paragraphs. Main ideas should not be buried in the middle of paragraphs or left to be inferred by the reader. (p. 53)

Considerate text also includes signal words or cue words that illustrate the relationships among the ideas. For example, words like *first*, *similarly*, *although*, *in contrast*, and *consequently* help readers recognize how ideas are related. (The *TRCA Teacher's Manual* offers a list of signal words authors use to help readers recognize how ideas are related.)

Based on this vision, some mathematics texts available for classroom use could be labeled "inconsiderate." For example, texts that are written as guided discovery can be more difficult for students to comprehend. In guided discovery, authors provide activities and questions through which students are supposed to discover the most important ideas or infer them on their own. Therefore, authors do not begin their discussion with a general topic sentence or thesis. Moreover, not all of the steps in their arguments are necessarily stated explicitly in the passage. Active participation in constructing meaning is essential; if students do not follow the logic of the author's ideas closely, they may miss the author's point.

Although guided discovery can be an effective instructional technique, novice readers may struggle with text written in this format. What if students do not make accurate inferences or reach the same conclusions that the author intends? And what if students cannot identify the main and supporting ideas? Research indicates that when the main idea of a passage is not clearly stated, even college-level readers have difficulty articulating it (Dickson et al., 1995). Therefore, we recommend that mathematics teachers preview their text to determine if the main ideas are clearly expressed and appear in a consistent location throughout the text.

Shuard and Rothery (1984) also note:

> In considering text as a whole, attention needs to be paid to the *clarity* and *flow of meaning* of the whole passage. Some mathematics text seems to stress obvious points while omitting important steps which the writer takes for granted, though their absence may prevent the reader from comprehending what is written. It is comparatively easy for the teacher to discover these gaps in the material he writes for his own classes, and to remedy omissions orally. The task of the published writer is more difficult, and the teacher should not take it for granted that, simply because material is published, it contains all the necessary explanation. . . . Clarity and flow of meaning are perhaps the most important features which enable pupils to "get the meaning from the page," and so to read mathematics with understanding. (p. 135)

In summary, whereas a text's macrostructure provides readers with a sense of how major sections of text are related, a text's microstructure — the methods the author uses to tie together ideas between sentences and paragraphs — helps readers identify which ideas are most important and distinguish those from information that develops, illustrates, or otherwise elaborates on those main ideas. As Readence et al. (2001) explain, "The relationships that bind together individual sentences in a text into a coherent structure comprise a text's *microstructure*" (p. 48). Unless these relationships are apparent to the reader, reading comprehension can suffer. Because both the macrostructure and microstructure of a text affect its coherence, it might be helpful for mathematics teachers to evaluate how each of these elements is apparent in their textbooks and how well each assists comprehension.

Audience Appropriateness

Ideally, the textbooks students are assigned to read are "audience appropriate" — that is, the text content matches students' probable prior knowledge base (Armbruster, 1996) and their ability to process and retain new information. Therefore, mathematics teachers need to select text that

- aligns with students' prior knowledge and experience;

- develops new concepts and processes at a reasonable pace; and

- uses language, phrasing, and sentence structure that students can understand.

Unfortunately, as we noted in the Rationale to this supplement, mathematics text often contains more concepts per paragraph and per page than any other content-area text. And, unlike narrative text in which authors often write elaborate descriptions or explanations, the content in mathematics text is written in a very compact style. Readers need to "unpack" meaning from mathematics text. Definitions are terse; a concept may be explained in one sentence, with little redundancy. These text features make reading mathematics a challenge even for able readers.

Text density is important in light of what cognitive psychologists tell us about human memory. Specifically, cognitive psychologists view memory in terms of short-term memory and long-term memory. Short-term memory is sometimes called "working memory" because it stores information temporarily until it is either processed into long-term memory or "deleted" as additional information is acquired (Readence et al., 2001).

It is this short-term memory that can be taxed when students read densely packed mathematics text. This is because short-term memory is both limited in its capacity to store a great deal of information and is, by its very nature, fleeting. As Readence et al. explain, "The single most important feature of short-term memory is its limited capacity for storing information" (p. 45). In fact, short-term memory can store only approximately seven individual pieces of information. Thus, even a 10-digit phone number can be difficult to retain, unless the learner "chunks" the information into fewer, more manageable bits.

However, even this chunking strategy cannot help learners overcome another aspect of short-term memory:

> The second important feature of short-term memory is its fleeting nature. Information such as a new friend's phone number must be constantly rehearsed if it is to remain available in short-term memory for longer than a few seconds. If attention is diverted for even a moment to something else, the limited storage capacity of short-term memory will be overloaded and the phone number erased to accept the new, incoming information. (Readence et al., 2001, p. 46)

Therefore, when less-able readers confront text that is very dense or that is written above their reading level, they have to read more slowly to make sense of the information. Short-term memory can become overburdened in the process, especially if readers must sound out unfamiliar words or attempt to construct meaning about abstract concepts. By the time readers reach the end of the sentence they are reading, they may have forgotten what they read at the beginning of the sentence.

McREL

Reading word problems can present similar challenges for mathematics students. Because these problems require readers to store details from one part of the problem while processing additional details at the same time, they can overburden the limited storage capacity of the readers' short-term memory (Readence et al., 2001).

In short, mathematics teachers should carefully select text material that is audience appropriate. It should be written at students' general reading level and should not contain too many abstract concepts for students to learn and retain in one reading.

Mathematics teachers can avoid potential problems with audience appropriateness not only by carefully selecting text that is targeted at their students' knowledge base and skill levels, but also by teaching students how to work with their textbook's organization, layout, and writing style. We encourage teachers to model for their students how to recognize and use text features that are meant to help readers make sense of, and learn from, mathematics text.

Section 2
Strategic Processing

Things to Think About

1. What techniques related to reading mathematics help students succeed in comprehending and learning from mathematics text?

2. What reading strategies help students interact with text and reflect on what they are reading?

3. What reading contexts can engage students and challenge them to apply what they have learned?

Because of the syntactic structure of its sentences and its specialized vocabulary, reading mathematics text requires a great deal of concentration. As Reehm and Long (1996) recommend, mathematics text needs to be read carefully and with a pencil and paper handy:

> Using paper and pencil while reading allows the student to perform the indicated computations, answer questions, or draw appropriate graphs or diagrams. This active application of text content during reading is essential for comprehension. Asking students to pause at designated points in the reading for group discussion, sharing, and clarification of concepts is also essential. (p. 38)

Reading a typical story problem requires considerable strategic processing skill. The student has to grasp the "big picture," or problem as a whole; concentrate on the main idea, which may not appear until the end of the problem; decide which formulas and computation procedures to use; and extract the relevant information and data that will help solve the problem on paper (Musthafa, 1996).

In addition to factual knowledge and skills, conceptual understanding is essential to mathematics. As NCTM (2000) declares, "Being proficient in a complex domain such as mathematics entails the ability to use knowledge flexibly, applying what is learned in one setting appropriately in another" (p. 20). NCTM recommends that students'

understanding of mathematics ideas be supported through their active engagement in tasks and experiences that are designed to deepen and connect their knowledge.

One method of challenging students to apply what they have learned is to have them read and write mathematics stories. In contrast to traditional story problems, math stories are complete narratives that focus on characters and their actions. The mathematics problems or applications grow out of the story line. Martinez and Martinez (2001) assert that such stories can draw students into "imaginative worlds of mathematics where ideas come alive" and where they can experience mathematics as more than "a cut-and-dried collection of unimaginable facts and formulas" (p. 51).

Martinez and Martinez describe a variety of math story genres teachers can use. One genre that can generate high interest is the math mystery. A math mystery asks student-sleuths to use basic, detective skills to solve a mathematics mystery. For instance, the case might require students to identify key elements in the case, look for patterns in events or things, infer solutions to the "case" based on evidence given, or identify inconsistencies or incongruities in what happens. The story, *A Valentine Mystery*, in Exhibit 11 is an example.

Exhibit 11. Math Mystery

A Valentine Mystery

Tomorrow is going to be a marvelous day; it is Valentine's Day. I called my best friend, the number Zero, to share my excitement.

"Tomorrow we will have a big party at school," I said. "We have made up strange songs, wild dances, new games and funny stories for the party. The school band will play and the theater will be decorated with large pictures that we have drawn ourselves. At the end of the celebrations, we will exchange valentines. It will be a great day!"

"In the World of Numbers, we have different customs for Valentine's Day," said Zero. "Each year, we challenge the human beings by inventing a game that can only be played by numbers."

I was puzzled.

Exhibit 11 (continued)

Notes

"What game did you invent?" I asked. "If you explain it to me clearly, I bet that tomorrow I can play it with my friends at school."

Zero laughed. "You poor human being! You don't seem to realize the power of the numbers."

I was confused and a little angry. "Zero is an interesting fellow," I thought. "But sometimes Zero is a show-off."

"I am the author of the new Valentine Game," said my friend. "I played it today with all of the whole numbers."

I started to listen very carefully.

"You know that I don't like to write letters but that I enjoy receiving lots of them," said my friend.

"That's true," I observed. "When you travel, you always forget to send me a postcard."

"I am lazy," agreed Zero. "But I like to make people happy. So in my new game:

> Each whole number sends exactly one valentine to a whole number
> and
> each whole number receives exactly ten valentines from ten whole numbers.

"You must be joking," I said. "Let us pretend that I play this game with all of the pupils in my class. There are 25 of us. If each person writes one letter, then altogether we send exactly 25 letters. But if each person has to receive 10 letters, we need 250 letters. Your game doesn't make any sense."

"Now slow down a minute," advised my friend. "Don't forget that we are not people. We are numbers. We are very powerful."

"That is easy to say," I replied. "But you will have to convince me that it is true."

"Okay," said Zero. "But I cannot do it on the phone. I will have to draw some pictures to make the game clear. Are you free tomorrow after school?"

"Yes. I shall expect you at 4 p.m."

"Bye, bye. Sleep well. Don't dream too much of my game."

The next day, at 4 p.m.

The doorbell rang. It was my friend carrying a bundle of posters. Zero was relaxed and very confident as usual. We put one of the posters on the floor.

Exhibit 11 (continued)

"Look and think," said Zero.

I was silent for a while.

"Do you understand the rule of my game?" asked Zero.

	Sends a valentine to	
0	→	0
6	→	0
27	→	2
85	→	8
349	→	34
506	→	50
4217	→	421
30672	→	3067

"You're a selfish number," I said laughingly. "You send a valentine to yourself and to nobody else in this game."

"That's true," agreed Zero. "But I only did it so that my game would succeed. Look carefully at the whole poster and try to find out something much more interesting."

"You receive a valentine from 6," I observed. "So you get at least two valentines."

"Don't think only of me," advised my friend.

"It's strange. It looks as though the numbers don't send their valentines to just anybody. There is some kind of pattern in your poster. But I don't completely inderstand it."

HOW ABOUT YOU?

Activities

1. Describe the rule of Zero's game, and give examples to show that each whole number sends just one valentine but receives ten.

2. Why does this game "work" with the whole numbers, but not with people?

3. Could you create a game where each whole number would send just one valentine but receive 100?

Note: From *A Valentine Mystery* (pp. 1–6), by F. Papy, 1986, a storybook in the Comprehensive School Mathematics Program, Aurora CO: McREL. Copyright 1986 by Mid-continent Research for Education and Learning.

Another genre of math story is the math fable, tall tale, or fairy tale. In this case, well-known fables, tall tales, or fairy tales are rewritten as math stories that include numbers or require computations. Exhibit 12 has an example of a math fable.

Exhibit 12. Math Fable

Achillies and the Tortoise

A long time ago in Ancient Greece, a trickster named Pan decided to play a joke on a warrior. The warrior's name was Achilles, and he liked to brag about how fast he could run.

"I'm the world's fastest runner," said Achilles.

"You're not so fast," replied Pan. "In fact, I know a tortoise who could race you and win."

Since tortoises are known for their slowness, that was an insult.

"I can beat any tortoise in any race," Achilles scoffed.

"Of course, there would have to be certain conditions," Pan said, trying to keep a straight face. "Otherwise, my tortoise-friend wouldn't agree to race."

"Doesn't matter," growled Achilles. "Any conditions. Any race. I'll beat the tortoise."

"And you'll have to make it worth his while," Pan added. "A tortoise can't race for nothing."

"Anything! Gold coins, jewels. You name it."

This is getting better and better, thought Pan. He set a time and a place for the race, then went looking for a tortoise to enter. He didn't really have a friend who was a tortoise. He had made that up.

He finally found a tortoise sunning himself on a rock.

"Me? Race Achilles? You're kidding," said the tortoise whose name was Tortilla.

"You'll have a head start," Pan assured him. "Achilles won't have a chance."

When it was time for the race, Pan explained his conditions. Tortilla would start 100 yards ahead of Achilles, and Achilles would only run 10 times as fast the tortoise.

"Huh?" said Achilles. He was beginning to get confused, but he agreed.

And they were off.

Exhibit 12 (continued)

Achilles ran 100 yards and reached the place where Tortilla started. Meanwhile the tortoise had gone 1/10 as far as Achilles and was therefore 10 yards ahead.

Achilles ran that 10 yards while Tortilla ran 1 yard. Then Achilles ran this 1 yard while the tortoise ran 1/10 of a yard. Achilles ran this 1/10 of a yard; Tortilla 1/10 of 1/10 of a yard, putting him 1/100 of a yard in front of Achilles. While Achilles ran this 1/100 of a yard, Tortilla was ahead by 1/1000 of a yard.

"It's working," laughed Pan. "Achilles is always getting closer to Tortilla, but he can never catch up!"

(Adapted from, Lancelot Hogben, *Mathematics for the Millions: How to Master the Magic of Numbers* [New York: W. W. Norton, 1993], p.11.)

Activities

1. What do you think? Did Pan's trick work? Will Achilles ever catch the tortoise? Will he have to pay Tortilla a forfeit of gold and jewels?

2. Do the math. Show how the tortoise wins or show the point where Achilles catches the tortoise.

3. Turn this story into a math play. Choose three classmates to play Pan, Achilles, and Tortilla. You may need to adjust the distances if your play takes place in the classroom—for example, the tortoise's head start could be 10 feet instead of 100 yards. Measure the distances, then mark them with the masking tape. Does acting out the story change your mind about who wins the race?

Note: From *Reading and Writing to Learn Mathematics: A Guide and Resource Book* (pp. 57–58), by J. G. R. Martinez and N. C. Martinez, 2001, Needham Heights, MA: Allyn & Bacon. Copyright 2001 by Allyn & Bacon. Reprinted by permission of Allyn & Bacon.

How math stories are presented and used in class will vary according to grade level. Exhibit 13 is a chart from Martinez and Martinez (2001) outlining an approach to using math stories in the classroom.

Exhibit 13. Learning with Math Stories by Grade Level

Methods	Grades K–2	Grades 3–4	Grades 5+
Presentation	Teacher reads aloud, illustrates with chalkboard drawings or cutouts.	Teacher and students read aloud, with time for questions and clarification.	Students read individually or in small groups, perhaps in conjunction with math journal activities.
Discussion	What's the story about? Did you like the story? What happens in the story? Which character did you like best? Least?	What kind of math did we find in the story? If the story goes on, what happens next? What do you think about the story?	What did you learn about math from this story? Is it a good story? Why do you think what happens happens?
Assignments	Talk through the math. Draw a picture to show what happened. Work out the math problems from the story with manipulatives.	Write explanations and comments. Identify concepts, processes, and patterns. Draw, act out, or apply ideas in hands-on activities.	Write through the math. Reflect on objectives, outcomes, and processes. Apply learning in reports and creative activities. Consider what happens if . . . ?

Note: From *Reading and Writing to Learn Mathematics: A Guide and Resource Book* (p. 67), by J. G. R. Martinez and N. C. Martinez, 2001, Needham Heights, MA: Allyn & Bacon. Copyright 2001 by Allyn & Bacon. Reprinted by permission of Allyn & Bacon.

Another resource teachers can use as the basis for real-life applications of learning is the newspaper. Newspaper stories often include a variety of mathematics references — percentages, fractions, measurements, geometric relationships, and statistics, to name just a few. The sports pages, science and technology sections, lifestyle pages, and business section offer numerous opportunities for students to extend and refine their understanding through estimating, calculating, manipulating, and, yes, questioning numerical data. Martinez and Martinez (2001) explain:

> In other words, the newspaper not only provides us with material for studying numbers and basic operations, but also for developing math sense, for exercising math thinking, and even for introducing more advanced mathematical ideas. Moreover, it does all this within a human context and in a story-based format. The result? High interest, relevance, and flexibility. (p. 141)

Exhibit 14 gives some of the mathematics content that might be found in different sections of the newspaper.

Exhibit 14. Math in the News

NEWS STORIES	OP/ED	SPECIAL FEATURES
Election results Poll statistics Catastrophic weather data War/refugee numbers and demographics Riot/protest numbers Magnitude of natural disasters Dollar losses for crime or disasters Gaming costs and income Maps of world hot spots	Data on bond issues Public spending Audits Historic dates Tuition hikes Tax hikes Land-use controversies Enviromental data	Measurements for do-it-yourself projects Patterns and measurements for sewing Match-makers/personal stats World/National records — biggest, smallest, oldest, youngest, farthest, heaviest Bridge strategies
SPORTS	**AD/CLASSIFIEDS**	**FOOD/DINING**
Scores Records Attendance numbers Rankings/Standings Batting averages Salaries Win/Loss numbers Race results Handicapping Distances, heights Weights, times	Ratios (cost/year) Addresses (whole numbers) Percentages "off" Measurements Dates Costs Fractions (1/2 off) Loan interest Quantities	Recipes Data about calories, cholesteral, fat, supplement USRDAs Serving sizes Restaurant ratings Nutrition info — grams of sodium, minerals, etc. Costs
TRAVEL/OUTDOORS	**ARTS**	**LOCAL**
Travel costs Lodging costs Dates Cruise-ship data and diagrams Sales Maps Equipment lists and specifications Survival supplies Passport info	Event times and places Project funding Publication data Best-seller lists Grants Cost/Fees	Local employment rate and salaries Tourism stats Election data Assets of elected officials Public spending Traffic numbers Crime numbers Polls

Exhibit 14 (continued)

FINANCIAL PAGES	HOME/REAL ESTATE	WEATHER/OBITS
Annuities Stocks Profits and losses Debt Interest rates Insurance Graphs and diagrams of data Market info Employment stats GNP figures Corporate reports Flowcharts	Floor plans Payment data (cost, estimated taxes, and insurance monthly payment) Loan rates Realtor's sales Area maps Addresses Phone numbers Square footage and dimensions	Temperatures Precipitation Humidity figures Pollen counts Solar/UV index Average precip Average temp Pollution index Wind speeds Weather map Dates/Ages Numbers in family Years of military, jobs, other service

ENTERTAINMENT	HEALTH
Ticket costs Dates and time VCR code number Ratings Channels	Statistical data from studies Health-risk projects Health-care costs Insurance/Medicare data Cholesterol levels Blood-sugar levels

Note: From *Reading and Writing to Learn Mathematics: A Guide and Resource Book* (pp. 142–143), by J. G. R. Martinez and N. C. Martinez, 2001, Needham Heights, MA: Allyn & Bacon. Copyright 2001 by Allyn & Bacon. Reprinted by permission of Allyn & Bacon.

Use these sources as the basis for activities that require students to extend and refine their understanding of mathematics concepts. Comparing, classifying, developing mathematical reasoning skills, constructing support for one's ideas, and analyzing and evaluating the mathematical thinking and strategies of others can extend and refine understanding. Naturally, instruction in these skills develops in complexity through the grades.

Borasi, Siegel, Fonzi, and Smith (1998) studied the effectiveness of a number of reading strategies when used in mathematics classes. Three of these strategies, Cloning An Author (Harste & Short, 1988), Using Cards, and Sketch-to-Stretch, help students to interact with the text and to process and reflect on what they are reading.

In Cloning An Author, students are asked to pause during reading whenever they encounter a key concept or important idea, and to summarize this concept or idea on a note card. When students finish reading and note taking, they are asked to arrange their cards in a way that shows the relationships among these ideas. Next, students share their note-card "maps" with their peers. As they discuss what they found to be important and why, students can rearrange their cards to reflect any new connections they have made as a result of the discussion.

Teachers in the Borasi et al. (1998) study developed a variation of this strategy, which they called "Using Cards." As in Cloning an Author, students take notes while they read; however, in Using Cards, students also record any comprehension problems they experience, questions that arise while reading, and connections they see between what they are reading and their prior knowledge. Instead of arranging these cards to show relationships among the ideas, students simply discuss their notes during a class discussion.

During the discussion that follows note taking in both of these strategies, students revisit and further explore text content, which helps them to confront what they didn't understand, restructure their schemata, and integrate their new learning into their knowledge base. Teachers also gain valuable insights from the students' cards. Because students turn in their note cards after the Using Cards discussion, teachers can review each student's comprehension of the content, evaluate participation level, and use this information to inform. their instruction.

In the Sketch-to-Stretch strategy, students are asked to draw a sketch representing what they learned and to explain their sketches to the class. According to Marzano et al. (2001), when students construct such "nonlinguistic representations," they are engaging in elaborative thought; furthermore, "When students elaborate on knowledge, they not only understand it in greater depth, but they can recall it much more easily" (p. 74). Moreover, when students are asked to explain and justify their elaboration, learning is extended and amplified.

When students created their sketches as part of the Borasi et al. (1998) study, students acknowledged that representing their learning in this symbolic fashion helped them better understand the material. Also, when students shared with their classmates how they viewed the content, new questions were generated and understanding extended as students compared the various ways their peers interpreted the text.

Strategic processing is essential to reading and learning. NCTM (2000) points out that a major goal of school mathematics programs is creating independent learners, and that learning with understanding supports that goal:

> Students learn more and learn better when they can take control of their learning by defining their goals and monitoring their progress. . . . Effective learners recognize the importance of reflecting on their thinking and learning from their mistakes. (p. 21)

Model for students how you monitor and reflect on your own understanding of new ideas. Then help students do the same.

In summary, mathematics teachers need to offer students a variety of opportunities to process what they are learning and to reflect on, refine, and extend their new learnings.

Section 3
Strategic Teaching

Things to Think About

1. What does strategic teaching in mathematics include?

2. Where in mathematics does the teaching of reading strategies belong?

Strategic teaching means being purposeful and thoughtful about planning instruction. Strategic teaching is a multistep process. It includes

- identifying a learning goal;

- considering how each student's prior knowledge, experience, learning style, and needs may affect their attainment of that goal;

- selecting appropriate instructional materials, activities, and strategies to help each student achieve the learning goal;

- developing the lesson plan;

- implementing the lesson plan;

- measuring the effectiveness of learning and instruction through assessment; and

- reviewing assessment data to inform future instruction.

Smith and Kepner (1981), the authors of *Reading in the Mathematics Classroom,* present an instructional framework that mathematics teachers may find useful when planning instruction (see Exhibit 15). The authors point out that their purpose is to present a comprehensive list of activities that teachers can use to select those they think will best support learning. Smith and Kepner also make the following important recommendation:

> Teachers who have been frustrated when students fail to read would do well to reconsider the directions they give when making an assignment. [We] urge teachers not to say, "Go read," but to give purpose and direction to the assignment. (p. 14)

Exhibit 15. Instructional Framework

Instructional Framework

I. Introductory Activities — student motivation, preparation, and direction

    A. Selecting appropriate motivational activities

        1. Inclusion of teacher-dominated or student-dominated activities

        2. Use of a media presentation

    B. Reviewing pertinent background information

        1. Teacher-led discussion of prior learnings

        2. Student awareness of learning as related to real-life situations

        3. Discussion of important concepts related to the lesson

    C. Setting purposes for the lesson

        1. Discuss with students the types of problems they will be solving.

        2. Give students a list of questions to answer as they do the lesson.

        3. Identify the types of follow-up activities students will perform.

    D. Giving directions for reading

        1. Discuss strategies useful in reading word problems.

        2. Identify key sentences or paragraphs in the text.

        3. Eliminate unnecessary reading passages.

        4. Set reasonable time limits for reading, problem solving, and follow-up activities.

        5. Discuss important tables, diagrams, and charts needed during the lesson.

    E. Teaching essential vocabulary

        1. List important terminology (words and symbols) on the chalkboard.

        2. Select representative words and symbols which will be taught for meaning or pronunciation or both.

        3. Pronounce remaining words and symbols for students.

II. Assimilation Activities — instruction in the major understandings

    A. Lecture style discussion

    B. Silent reading

    C. Supplementary instruction (e.g., media presentation)

    D. Supervised study

    E. Guided discovery lesson

III. Follow-up Activities — activities intended to extend, internalize, or reinforce student learning

    A. Small group discussions

    B. Teacher-made content tests

    C. Vocabulary games or puzzles

    D. Mathematical project (individual or group)

    E. Additional teaching in the meaning or pronunciation of words and symbols

    F. Demonstrations of the mathematical principle being studied in different contexts

    G. Written assignments

    H. Model construction

    I. Additional practice in reading word problems

    J. Additional instruction in strategies useful in solving word problems

    K. Discussion of related student experiences

    L. Additional reading or study in supplementary textbooks

Note: From *Reading in the Mathematics Classroom* (pp. 13–14), by C. F. Smith and H. S. Kepner, Jr. (with R. B. Kane), 1981, Washington, DC: National Education Association. Copyright 1981 by National Education Association. Reprinted with permission.

McREL

In her chapter "Strategic Teaching in Mathematics," Lindquist (1987) offers a Planning Guide for Strategic Teaching in Mathematics (see Exhibit 16). This guide is a resource mathematics teachers might find helpful in designing lessons that encourage students to use thinking and metacognitive skills as they learn mathematics skills, concepts, and problem solving.

Exhibit 16. Planning Guide for Strategic Teaching in Mathematics

PREPARING THE CONTENT

Assess level of learner
    set expectations

Discuss goal
    discuss nature of task
    model/elicit criteria for success

Preview problem/learning experience
    model guide preview (e.g., examine pictorial clues/content)

Activate background knowledge
    elicit background concepts and procedures
    confront misconceptions
    elicit strategies and plans

Focus direction/interest
    provide hints or structured activities
    model interest and clarify purpose

PRESENTING THE CONTENT

Pause/reflect
    model/guide planning
    elicit/discuss faulty logic, contradictions

Initiate action
    monitor progress (give hints if necessary)

Assimilate ideas
    discuss progress, change direction if necessary, give extension
    guide articulation

APPLYING/INTEGRATING

Integrate/organize
    share and discuss solutions and execution
    compare to "model" solutions and other learning experiences

Assess achievement
    model and discuss evaluation
    discuss old misconceptions
    provide reinforcement

Extend learning
    provide extensions of increased diversity and complexity
    discuss growth

Note: From "Strategic Teaching in Mathematics," by M. M. Lindquist, in *Strategic Teaching and Learning: Cognitive Instruction in the Content Areas* (p. 132), by B. F. Jones, A.S. Palincsar, D. S. Ogle, and E.G. Carr (Eds.), 1987, Alexandria, VA: Association for Supervision and Curriculum Development in cooperation with North Central Regional Educational Laboratory. Copyright 1987 by the North Central Regional Educational Laboratory. Reprinted with permission.

Notes

Lindquist offers the example shown in Exhibit 17 (not intended as a complete lesson plan) to illustrate how the planning guide might look in an eighth-grade class learning some geometry concepts.

Exhibit 17. Application of the Mathematics Planning Guide

PREPARING THE CONTENT

Assess level of learner: Students are familiar with some special quadrilaterals (squares, rectangles, parallelograms) and their properties. In fact, they may recognize some quadrilaterals as rhombuses.

Discuss goal: Announce to the students that they are going to learn about a special quadrilateral, the rhombus, adding it to their knowledge of polygons.

Preview problem: Decide what there is to learn about the rhombus, generating a list of questions and characteristics.

Activate background knowledge: Ask students to generate the list of properties from what they know about squares, rectangles, and parallelograms.

Quadrilaterals

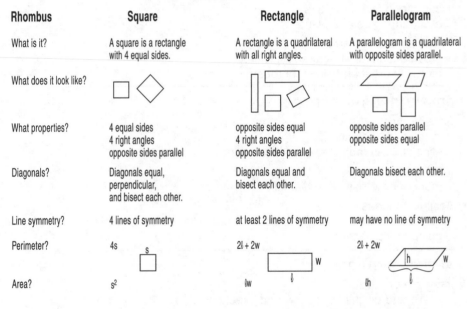

	Rhombus	Square	Rectangle	Parallelogram
What is it?		A square is a rectangle with 4 equal sides.	A rectangle is a quadrilateral with all right angles.	A parallelogram is a quadrilateral with opposite sides parallel.
What does it look like?				
What properties?		4 equal sides 4 right angles opposite sides parallel	opposite sides equal 4 right angles opposite sides parallel	opposite sides parallel opposite sides equal
Diagonals?		Diagonals equal, perpendicular, and bisect each other.	Diagonals equal and bisect each other.	Diagonals bisect each other.
Line symmetry?		4 lines of symmetry	at least 2 lines of symmetry	may have no line of symmetry
Perimeter?		$4s$	$2\ell + 2w$	$2\ell + 2w$
Area?		s^2	ℓw	ℓh

Focus direction: Two at a time, present sketches of polygons, one that is a rhombus and one that is not.

Rhombus

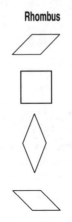

Not a Rhombus

McREL

Exhibit 17 (continued)

PRESENTING THE CONTENT

Pause/reflect: Examine the examples and nonexamples of rhombuses to determine the distinguishing characteristics. Decide why each nonexample is not a rhombus. Define a rhombus.

Solicit from students a relationship between squares and rhombuses, or between parallelograms and rhombuses.

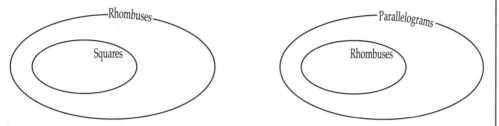

Initiate action: When students are clear about what a rhombus is, let groups investigate properties such as those related to diagonals, symmetry, perimeter, and area. Each group might picture several different rhombuses and answer questions such as:

Do all rhombuses have diagonals of equal length?
Do any rhombuses have diagonals of equal length?
How many lines of symmetry does a rhombus have?
How can you find the perimeter (the area) of a rhombus?

Assimilate ideas: Let groups report their findings and tell how they arrived at the results. Discuss any questions that arose in the groups.

APPLYING/INTEGRATING

Integrate/organize: Review the relationships between the properties of the four special quadrilaterals. How are squares like rhombuses; how are rhombuses like parallelograms; how are rectangles different from rhombuses?

A graphic organizer can present the information:

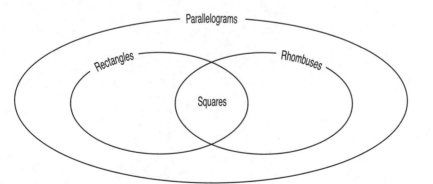

Extend learning: Some students may be ready to extend the investigation to include trapezoids and kites.

Note: Adapted from "Strategic Teaching in Mathematics," by M. M. Lindquist, in *Strategic Teaching and Learning: Cognitive Instruction in the Content Areas* (p. 124–127), by B. F. Jones, A.S. Palincsar, D. S. Ogle, and E.G. Carr (Eds.), 1987, Alexandria, VA: Association for Supervision and Curriculum Development in cooperation with North Central Regional Educational Laboratory. Copyright 1987 by the North Central Regional Educational Laboratory. Adapted with permission.

McREL

Notes

Clearly, strategic teaching encompasses more than the teaching of reading in mathematics. However, content instruction should be the venue in which reading strategy instruction occurs, rather than in some isolated fashion set apart from the teaching of content.

Section 4
Six Assumptions About Learning

Six Assumptions About Learning

Learning is
1. goal oriented.
2. the linking of new information to prior knowledge.
3. the organization of information.
4. the acquisition of cognitive and metacognitive structures.
5. in phases, yet is nonlinear.
6. influenced by cognitive development.

Recent research about student learning emphasizes learning for understanding. This research provides insights that can strengthen the link between what researchers know about learning and what happens in the classroom.

Jones, Palincsar, Ogle, and Carr (1987) have proposed six assumptions about how students learn. Because these assumptions stem from significant research and have important implications for reading, including reading in mathematics, they warrant study by educators who want to examine how learning theory aligns with and undergirds reading theory. (These assumptions are discussed in more depth in Section 4 of the *TRCA Teacher's Manual*, pp. 61–67.)

Assumption 1: Learning is goal oriented.
Skilled learners have two goals: to construct meaning and to become self-directed, autonomous learners. Learning for understanding supports these goals. Reading in mathematics is not a passive activity; it is the active construction of meaning by learners. Problem solving, inquiry, and reading all should involve the processes of planning, monitoring, evaluating comprehension, making inferences, drawing conclusions, revising schema, extending and refining knowledge, and analyzing information based on prior knowledge. These processes help learners construct meaning and take control of their learning. Simply doing a routine mathematics procedure or engaging in reading as merely a word-calling exercise does not help students construct meaning or take control of their learning.

Assumption 2: Learning is the linking of new information to prior knowledge.

Students bring to a learning experience their current understandings, attitudes, and abilities. They have conceptions and sometimes misconceptions about the world of mathematics, both of which influence their learning. Students' understanding of mathematical ideas can be built throughout their school years if they actively engage in tasks and experiences designed to deepen and connect their knowledge (NCTM, 2000). Textbooks, however, are often set up in a "tell-and-verify" format; students are expected to read about mathematics concepts and then do exercises that verify or require them to use what they have just read. Providing students with opportunities to explore worthwhile mathematics tasks before and after reading can give students the chance to have concepts reinforced, confirmed, or enriched as they read about them.

Assumption 3: Learning involves organizing information.

Realizing that authors of informational text (textbooks or trade books) organize information in a variety of ways can help learners make meaning of what they have read. Similarly, helping students make connections between the mathematics activities they are doing and their reading about mathematics can aid their understanding of mathematics concepts.

Assumption 4: Learning is the acquisition of cognitive and metacognitive structures.

Strategic learners are aware of their learning styles and are able to select and regulate their use of learning skills and strategies. Strategic processing is discussed more fully in Section 2 of this supplement (see pages 39–49).

Assumption 5: Learning occurs in phases, yet is nonlinear.

Costa and Garmston (1994) and Buehl (1995) believe that learning has three phases: preactive thought, interactive thought, and reflective thought. Preactive thought involves preparing for learning;

interactive thought (or processing) occurs during learning; and reflective thought involves integrating, extending, refining, and applying what has been learned. Strategies found in Section 5 of this supplement are identified by the appropriate phase.

Assumption 6: Learning is influenced by cognitive development.
Not all students arrive at school with the same set of knowledge and skills. Effective readers may have their own reading strategies; other readers may benefit from learning additional reading strategies; and poor readers may not be aware that there are strategies to help with understanding.

The following section is a toolkit of strategies designed to increase students' conceptual understanding of mathematics. Strategies are classified as vocabulary development (including symbolic vocabulary games), informational text, and reflection strategies. They are also identified as preactive (preparation before reading), interactive (assistance during reading), and/or reflective (reflection after reading).

Section 5
Reading Strategies

M-1. Concept Circles

What is it?

Concept circles (Vacca & Vacca, 1999) is a versatile categorization strategy for students to study words or terms critically, relating them conceptually to one another. With a concept circle, students identify common attributes or a concept relationship that exists among several terms. This may be a pre-reading activity to introduce new vocabulary concepts or an activity intended to reinforce and extend the knowledge of a concept.

How could it be used in mathematics instruction?

As a pre-reading activity, concept circles can involve students in predicting and discovering relationships, beginning the process of defining a concept. As a reinforcement or extension activity, students identify a concept (perhaps more than one) that relates several terms, thinking about common attributes and extensions.

How to use it:

1. Choose common attributes or relationships among a number of terms.

2. Draw a circle divided into sections (three to six) and put a term (word or phrase) into each section, all of which have the identified attributes or are related in a similar way.

3. Direct students to identify the common attributes or name the relationship that exists among the terms in all sections of the circle.

One modification of this strategy is to leave a section of the circle empty and direct students both to identify the concept relating all the terms given in the other sections and to fill in the empty section with a new term that also fits with this concept.

Another modification is to choose a term for just one section of the circle that is *not* an example of a concept and terms for all the other sections that are examples. Then direct students to find the term that does not belong and identify the concept that relates the other terms.

Vocabulary Development

Concept: <u>Conic Sections</u>

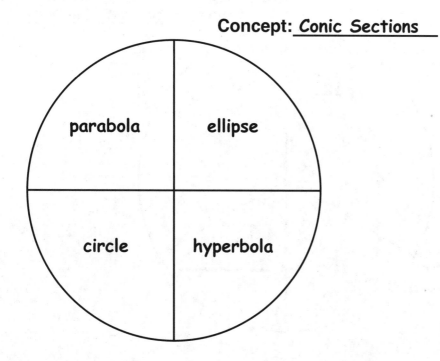

Concept: <u>Linear Equations</u>

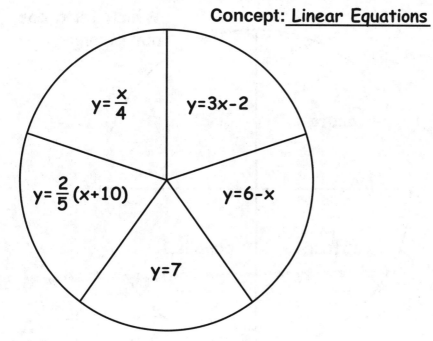

Notes

Vocabulary Development

Concept: <u>Square Numbers</u>

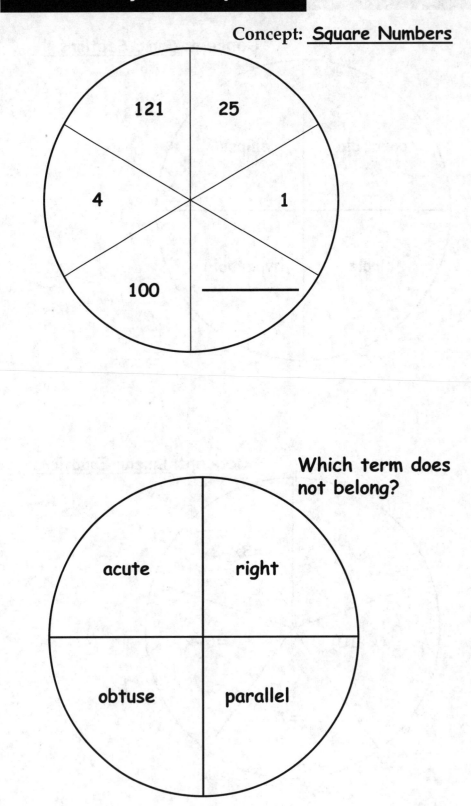

121	25
4	1
100	___

Which term does not belong?

acute	right
obtuse	parallel

Vocabulary Development

M-2. Concept Definition Mapping

What is it?

Concept definition mapping (Schwartz, 1988) is a strategy for teaching students the meaning of key concepts. Concept definition maps are graphic organizers that help students understand the essential attributes, qualities, or characteristics of a concept. Students must describe what the concept is, make comparisons, tell what it is like (what properties it has), and cite examples of it.

How could it be used in mathematics instruction?

This strategy provides a structure for students to organize their understanding after they have completed several activities using a concept and/or reading about the concept. It gives students an opportunity to communicate their understanding and to elaborate or make connections by citing examples from their own experiences.

How to use it:

1. Display an example of a concept definition map.

2. Discuss the questions that a definition should answer:

   - What is it? What broader category does it fit into?
   - What can it be compared to?
   - What is it like? What are its properties? What qualities make it different from other things in the same category?
   - What are some examples of it?

3. Model how to use the map.

4. Select concepts, or let students choose terms with which to practice.

5. Instruct students to use the information from their maps to write a complete definition of the concept.

6. As a unit progresses, encourage students to refine their maps and to reflect on their learning with additional properties and examples.

For further discussion on this strategy, see the *TRCA Teacher's Manual*, pp. 70–73.

Vocabulary Development

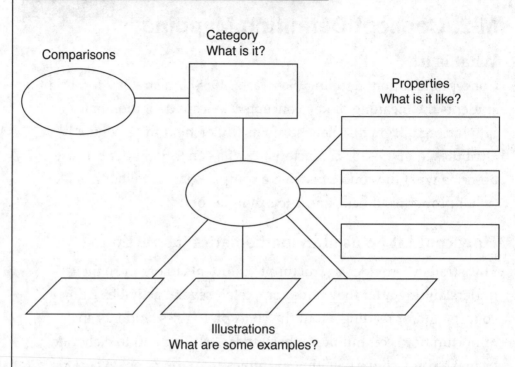

Note: From "Learning to Learn Vocabulary in Content Area Textbooks," by R. M. Schwartz, 1988, *Journal of Reading, 32,* p. 113. Copyright 1988 by the International Reading Association. Reprinted with permission.

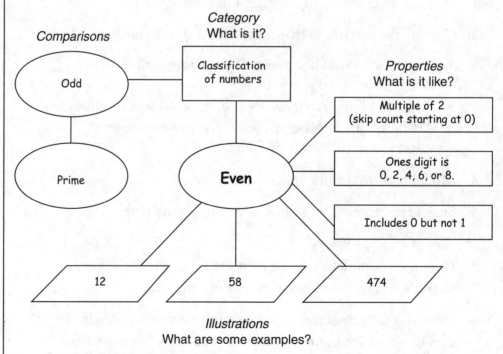

Note: Basic format only from "Learning to Learn Vocabulary in Content Area Textbooks," by R. M. Schwartz, 1988, *Journal of Reading, 32*, p. 113. Copyright 1988 by the International Reading Association.

Vocabulary Development

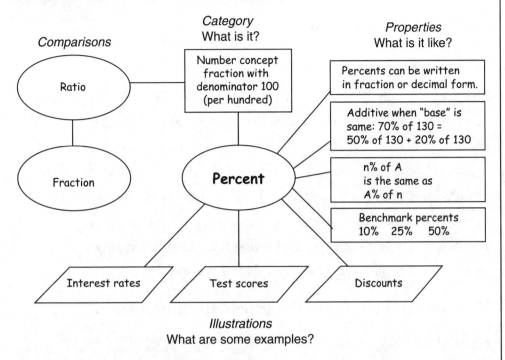

Comparisons

Category
What is it?

Properties
What is it like?

Ratio

Number concept
fraction with
denominator 100
(per hundred)

Percents can be written
in fraction or decimal form.

Additive when "base" is
same: 70% of 130 =
50% of 130 + 20% of 130

Fraction

Percent

n% of A
is the same as
A% of n

Benchmark percents
10% 25% 50%

Interest rates

Test scores

Discounts

Illustrations
What are some examples?

Note: Basic format only from "Learning to Learn Vocabulary in Content Area Textbooks," by R. M. Schwartz, 1988, *Journal of Reading, 32,* p. 113. Copyright 1988 by the International Reading Association.

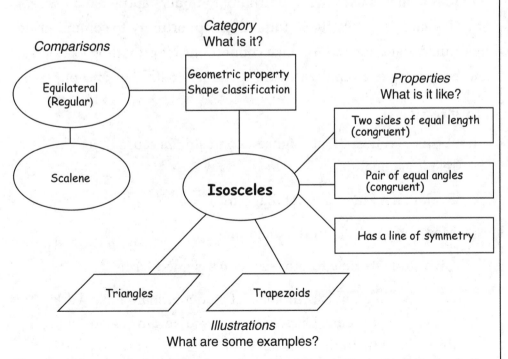

Comparisons

Category
What is it?

Equilateral
(Regular)

Geometric property
Shape classification

Properties
What is it like?

Two sides of equal length
(congruent)

Scalene

Isosceles

Pair of equal angles
(congruent)

Has a line of symmetry

Triangles

Trapezoids

Illustrations
What are some examples?

Note: Basic format only from "Learning to Learn Vocabulary in Content Area Textbooks," by R. M. Schwartz, 1988, *Journal of Reading, 32,* p. 113. Copyright 1988 by the International Reading Association.

 MCREL

Notes

M-3. Frayer Model

What is it?

The Frayer model (Frayer, Frederick, & Klausmeier, 1969) is a word categorization activity that helps learners develop their understanding of concepts. Two versions of the Frayer model are included in this manual. In the first, students provide a definition, list characteristics or facts, and provide examples and nonexamples of the concept. In the second, students analyze some essential and nonessential characteristics of a concept, and refine their understanding by choosing examples and nonexamples of the concept.

How could it be used in mathematics instruction?

There are many concepts in mathematics that can be confusing because of their close relationships (e.g., prime numbers and factors) and/or their specialized features (e.g., functions). This strategy provides students with the opportunity to understand what a concept is and what it is not. It gives students an opportunity to communicate their understanding and to make connections by providing examples and nonexamples from their own experiences with the concept.

How to use it:

1. Assign a concept that might be confusing because of its relational qualities.

2. Explain the Frayer model diagram.

3. Model how to fill out the diagram.

4. Give students time to practice with assigned terms.

5. Once the diagram is complete, let students share their work with other students. Display students' diagrams as posters throughout the unit so students can refer to the words and continue to add ideas.

For further discussion of this strategy, see the *TRCA Teacher's Manual,* pp. 74–77.

Vocabulary Development

<table>
<tr><td>**Definition** (in own words)</td><td>**Facts/Characteristics**</td></tr>
<tr><td colspan="2" align="center">**WORD**</td></tr>
<tr><td>**Examples**</td><td>**Nonexamples**</td></tr>
</table>

Note: From *A Schema for Testing the Level of Concept Mastery* (Working Paper No. 16), by D. A. Frayer, W. C. Frederick, and H. G. Klausmeier, 1969, Madison, WI: University of Wisconsin Research and Development Center for Cognitive Learning. Copyright 1969 by the University of Wisconsin. Reprinted with permission.

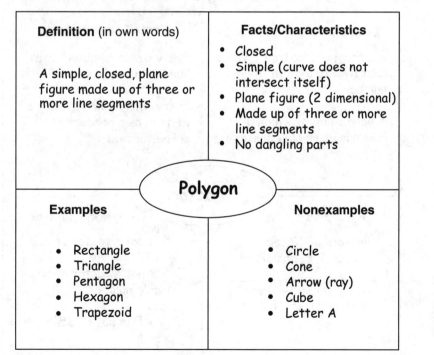

Definition (in own words)	**Facts/Characteristics**
A simple, closed, plane figure made up of three or more line segments	• Closed • Simple (curve does not intersect itself) • Plane figure (2 dimensional) • Made up of three or more line segments • No dangling parts
Polygon	
Examples	**Nonexamples**
• Rectangle • Triangle • Pentagon • Hexagon • Trapezoid	• Circle • Cone • Arrow (ray) • Cube • Letter A

Note: Basic format only from *A Schema for Testing the Level of Concept Mastery* (Working Paper No. 16), by D. A. Frayer, W. C. Frederick, and H. G. Klausmeier, 1969, Madison, WI: University of Wisconsin Research and Development Center for Cognitive Learning. Copyright 1969 by the University of Wisconsin.

Vocabulary Development

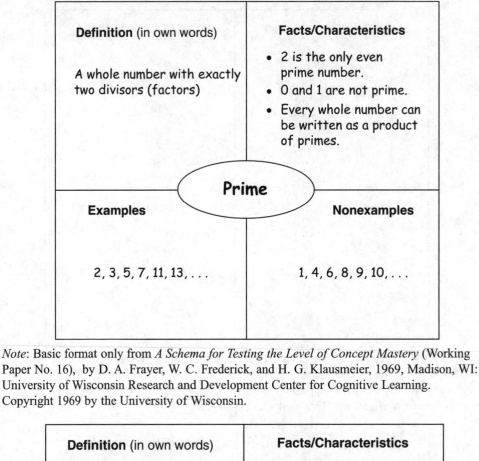

Definition (in own words)

A whole number with exactly two divisors (factors)

Facts/Characteristics

- 2 is the only even prime number.
- 0 and 1 are not prime.
- Every whole number can be written as a product of primes.

Prime

Examples

2, 3, 5, 7, 11, 13, . . .

Nonexamples

1, 4, 6, 8, 9, 10, . . .

Note: Basic format only from *A Schema for Testing the Level of Concept Mastery* (Working Paper No. 16), by D. A. Frayer, W. C. Frederick, and H. G. Klausmeier, 1969, Madison, WI: University of Wisconsin Research and Development Center for Cognitive Learning. Copyright 1969 by the University of Wisconsin.

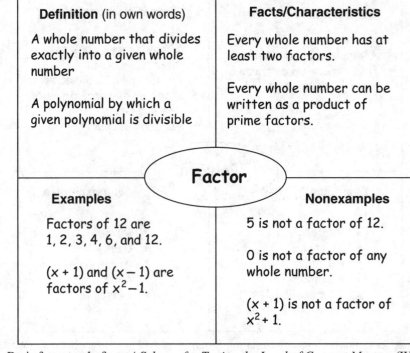

Definition (in own words)

A whole number that divides exactly into a given whole number

A polynomial by which a given polynomial is divisible

Facts/Characteristics

Every whole number has at least two factors.

Every whole number can be written as a product of prime factors.

Factor

Examples

Factors of 12 are 1, 2, 3, 4, 6, and 12.

$(x + 1)$ and $(x - 1)$ are factors of $x^2 - 1$.

Nonexamples

5 is not a factor of 12.

0 is not a factor of any whole number.

$(x + 1)$ is not a factor of $x^2 + 1$.

Note: Basic format only from *A Schema for Testing the Level of Concept Mastery* (Working Paper No. 16), by D. A. Frayer, W. C. Frederick, and H. G. Klausmeier, 1969, Madison, WI: University of Wisconsin Research and Development Center for Cognitive Learning. Copyright 1969 by the University of Wisconsin.

McREL

Vocabulary Development

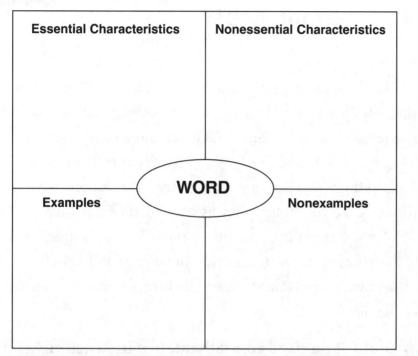

Note: From *A Schema for Testing the Level of Concept Mastery* (Working Paper No. 16), by D. A. Frayer, W. C. Frederick, and H. G. Klausmeier, 1969, Madison, WI: University of Wisconsin Research and Development Center for Cognitive Learning. Copyright 1969 by the University of Wisconsin. Reprinted with permission.

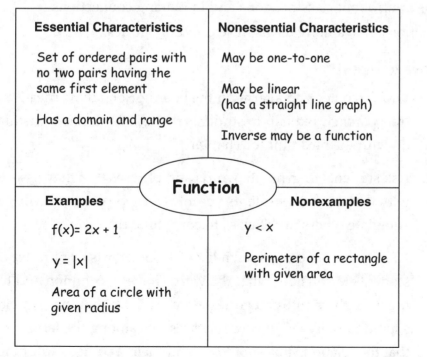

Note: Basic format only from *A Schema for Testing the Level of Concept Mastery* (Working Paper No. 16), by D. A. Frayer, W. C. Frederick, and H. G. Klausmeier, 1969, Madison, WI: University of Wisconsin Research and Development Center for Cognitive Learning. Copyright 1969 by the University of Wisconsin.

McREL

Vocabulary Development

M-4. List-Group-Label

What is it?

Similar to semantic mapping and word sort (pages 77 and 86 of this supplement), list-group-label helps students examine the relationships among subject-matter concepts. Taba, Durkin, Fraenkel, and McNaughton (1971) and Fraenkel (1973) note that this involves students in their own learning because they are responsible for contributing the vocabulary they associate with a particular concept rather than manipulating vocabulary provided by the teacher. As such, this strategy can activate prior knowledge and help learners make essential connections between their experience base and new understandings.

How could it be used in mathematics instruction?

This strategy is very effective in assessing students' prior knowledge and classification skills. It may be used to involve students in reasoning about classifications and in making connections (relationships) among terms in selected categories.

How to use it:

1. Write a content-area term on the board or on an overhead transparency. Explain to students that this term has something to do with the next unit (or chapter).

2. Ask students to generate words and phrases that they associate with this term. As students volunteer responses, they will stimulate others in the class to contribute their ideas.

3. After you have developed a list of 15–30 words or phrases, ask students to consider what the words have in common and to organize them into categories. Remind them that these categories should identify significant relationships among the terms, and that the relationships should extend their learning. Grouping words by their initial letter, for example, is not an activity that identifies a mathematically significant relationship.

Vocabulary Development

4. Once students have completed classifying these terms, ask them to explain the rationale behind their groupings. Small group work is likely to generate different categories, and class discussion of the differences can deepen understanding of the concepts.

5. Use this discussion as an opportunity to broaden students' understanding of these concepts and how to apply this understanding when solving problems.

Term: Measurement

Student-Generated List

weight	height	meter	length
foot	pound	mile	width
tape measure	circumference	area	perimeter
scale	radius	distance	ruler
age	quart	time	temperature
cup	yard	kilogram	thermometer

Categorize

Units of Measure	Things You Measure	Tools for Measurement
foot	weight	tape measure
pound	age	scale
yard	height	cup
quart	circumference	ruler
meter	radius	thermometer
mile	area	
kilogram	distance	
	time	
	length	
	width	
	perimeter	
	temperature	

Vocabulary Development

M-5. Semantic Feature Analysis

What is it?

Semantic feature analysis (Baldwin, Ford, & Readence, 1981; Johnson & Pearson, 1984) helps students discern a term's meaning by comparing its features to those of other terms that fall into the same category. When students have completed a semantic feature matrix, they have a visual reminder of how certain terms are alike or different.

How could it be used in mathematics instruction?

This strategy is very effective when examining discriminating features (e.g., when categorizing geometric shapes or numbers). This strategy can be used to engage students' thinking, as a way to collect data while students reason and communicate about similarities and differences, or as a way to quickly assess students' knowledge. When students add terms to the matrix, they are problem solving to find a term that has certain properties but not others.

How to use it:

1. Select a general category of study.

2. Create a matrix. Along the left side, list key terms in the chosen category. Across the top of the matrix, write features (properties) that these terms might share.

3. Ask students to use an "X" to indicate when a property applies to the term or to write in specifics about the features.

4. Encourage students to explain the rationale behind their choices.

5. As the unit progresses and understanding of each term or concept deepens, the teacher or students can add terms and features (properties) to the matrix.

For further discussion of this strategy, see the TRCA *Teacher's Manual*, pp. 79–81.

Vocabulary Development

Semantic Feature Analysis Grid

Category:

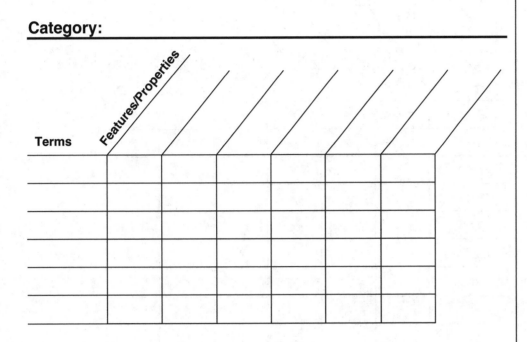

Category: Polygons

Terms	convex	equilateral	equiangular	4-sided	3-sided	opposite sides parallel
square	X	X	X	X		X
rectangle	X		X	X		X
triangle	X				X	
quadrilateral				X		
regular polygon	X	X	X			
rhombus	X	X		X		X
trapezoid	X			X		

Vocabulary Development

Category: Whole Numbers

Terms / Features/Properties	prime	perfect	deficient	abundant	square	triangular
3	X		X			X
6		X				X
7	X		X			
8			X			
9			X		X	
12				X		
16			X		X	
28		X				X
36				X	X	X

Category: Quadrilaterals

Terms / Features/Properties	diagonals are congruent	diagonals are perpendicular	diagonals bisect each other	all sides are congruent	all angles are congruent
parallelogram			X		
rhombus		X	X	X	
square	X	X	X	X	X
rectangle	X		X		X
trapezoid					
kite		X			

M-6. Semantic Mapping

What is it?

A semantic map is a visual tool that helps readers activate and draw on prior knowledge, recognize important components of different concepts, and see the relationships among these components.

How could it be used in mathematics instruction?

This strategy can be incorporated into the introduction of a topic to activate students' prior knowledge and then used throughout a unit or series of lessons on the topic. Students will be able to visualize how terms are connected and/or related. This strategy can be used to build connections between hands-on activities and reading activities.

How to use it:

1. Write the major topic of the lesson or unit on chart paper.

2. Let students brainstorm a list of terms that relate in some way to this major topic.

3. Write the major topic in the center of another sheet of chart paper and circle it.

4. Ask students to review the brainstormed list and begin to categorize the terms. The categories and terms should be discussed and then displayed in the form of a map or web.

5. Leave the chart up throughout the series of lessons or unit so that new categories and terms can be added as needed.

For further discussion of this strategy, see the *TRCA Teacher's Manual*, pp. 82–84.

Vocabulary Development

Form for Semantic Map

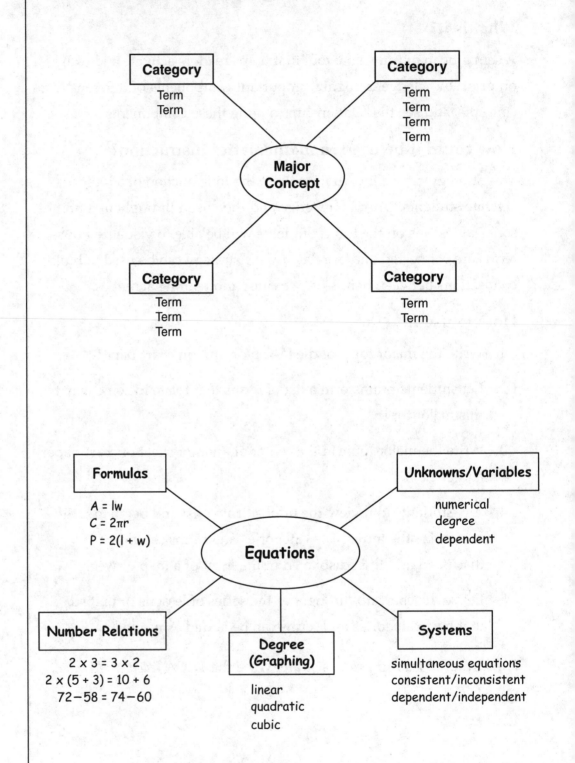

Vocabulary Development

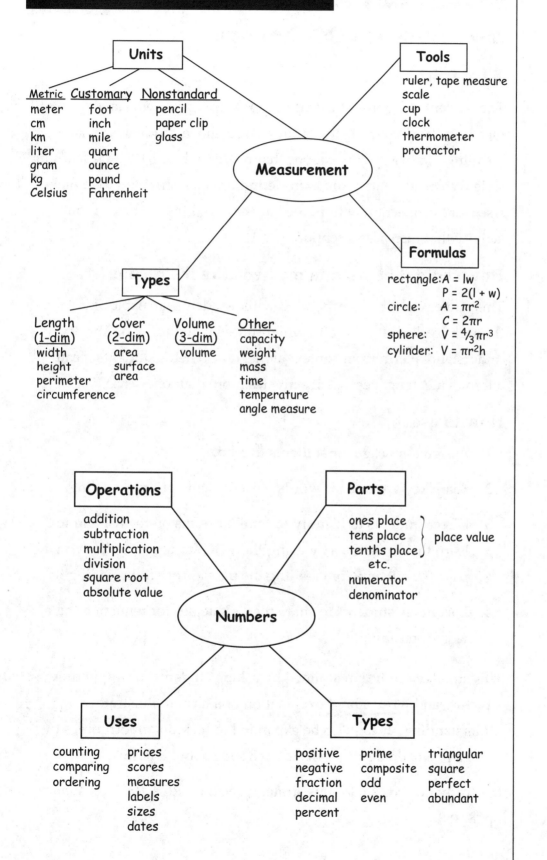

Units

Metric   Customary   Nonstandard
meter   foot   pencil
cm   inch   paper clip
km   mile   glass
liter   quart
gram   ounce
kg   pound
Celsius   Fahrenheit

Tools

ruler, tape measure
scale
cup
clock
thermometer
protractor

Measurement

Formulas

rectangle: A = lw
           P = 2(l + w)
circle: A = πr²
           C = 2πr
sphere: V = ⁴⁄₃πr³
cylinder: V = πr²h

Types

Length   Cover   Volume   Other
(1-dim)   (2-dim)   (3-dim)   capacity
width   area   volume   weight
height   surface   mass
perimeter area   time
circumference   temperature
                              angle measure

Operations

addition
subtraction
multiplication
division
square root
absolute value

Parts

ones place ⎫
tens place ⎬ place value
tenths place⎭
    etc.
numerator
denominator

Numbers

Uses

counting   prices
comparing scores
ordering   measures
           labels
           sizes
           dates

Types

positive prime   triangular
negative composite square
fraction odd   perfect
decimal   even   abundant
percent

M-7. Student VOC Strategy

What is it?

The student VOC strategy is useful for helping students analyze word meanings from context. The strategy also allows students to make meaningful sensory connections that relate to their particular learning style. When students write their definition for a term and then make a sensory connection with it, they are engaged in a "whole" brain activity that increases retention.

How could it be used in mathematics instruction?

This strategy can be incorporated while students are exploring through reading. It is helpful when students might not be able to understand a term from context alone. It also helps students recall a term's meaning, because it activates more than one sense.

How to use it:

1. Assign a passage for students to read.

2. Share key vocabulary words with students prior to reading.

3. Direct students to identify unfamiliar terms on the list and to learn their meanings by using the VOC strategy (see form on page 81) either before reading the passage or while reading it.

4. Encourage students to share their strategies for remembering a word's meaning.

This strategy can be streamlined by asking students to simply draw a picture and write a brief explanation of a term to illustrate understanding. It can also be expanded to include opportunities to write a poem, do a skit, or make up a song about a term.

For further discussion of this strategy, see the *TRCA Teacher's Manual,* pp. 87–88.

Vocabulary Development

Student VOC Strategy

Vocabulary Word: _____

1. Write the sentence in which it appears in the text:

   _____

   _____

2. Based upon how it is used in the text, predict what the word means:

   _____

3. Consult an "expert" for the actual definition (e.g., a friend, teacher, text

   resource). Expert: _____

   Expert's definition: _____

   _____

   _____

4. Show your understanding of the word by using it in a sentence of your

   own: _____

   _____

   _____

5. Choose one of the following ways to help you remember the word's meaning:
   Draw a picture of what the word means to you; select and perform a miming
   action that the word reminds you of; or connect the word with something
   similar that you've heard — in a story, a news report, or a song. Write down
   an association or connection you have made: _____

   _____

6. Explain why you chose this way to represent what the word means to you:

   _____

   _____

Vocabulary Development

Student VOC Strategy

Vocabulary Word: Circumference

1. Write the sentence in which it appears in the text:

    The garden includes a circular walkway with a circumference of 38 meters.

2. Based upon how it is used in the text, predict what the word means:

    The distance from one side of a circle to the other

3. Consult an "expert" for the actual definition (e.g., a friend, teacher, text resource). Expert: Teacher

    Expert's definition: The distance around (the boundary of) a circle

4. Show your understanding of the word by using it in a sentence of your own: I use the circumference of my finger to find my ring size, because the size is the distance around my finger.

5. Choose one of the following ways to help you remember the word's meaning: Draw a picture of what the word means to you; select and perform a miming action that the word reminds you of; or connect the word with something similar that you've heard — in a story, a news report, or a song. Write down an association or connection you have made:

6. Explain why you chose this way to represent what the word means to you:

    This picture reminds me that circumference is the distance around a circle.

Student VOC Strategy

Vocabulary Word: __Scale Factor__

1. Write the sentence in which it appears in the text:
   Use a scale factor greater than 1 to enlarge the diagram.

2. Based upon how it is used in the text, predict what the word means:
   A multiplier

3. Consult an "expert" for the actual definition (e.g., a friend, teacher, text resource). Expert: __Text__
   Expert's definition: The factor by which all parts of an object are multiplied to create a proportional enlargement or reduction

4. Show your understanding of the word by using it in a sentence of your own: Using a scale factor of 3 on a 2" by 2" square will result in a 6" x 6" square. Using a scale factor of ½ will result in a 1" by 1" square.

5. Choose one of the following ways to help you remember the word's meaning: Draw a picture of what the word means to you; select and perform a miming action that the word reminds you of; or connect the word with something similar that you've heard — in a story, a news report, or a song. Write down an association or connection you have made: In → Scale Factor Machine → Out

6. Explain why you chose this way to represent what the word means to you:
   I think of a scale factor as a machine because it "works" on anything put in it the same way — all parts are multiplied by the same amount.

M-8. Verbal and Visual Word Association (VVWA)

What is it?

The VVWA strategy puts together in a graphic a vocabulary word and its definition with both a visual of the term and a personal association or characteristic of the term. This strategy helps students learn vocabulary on their own and helps them retain the new vocabulary through visual characteristic associations. This strategy has been shown to be especially effective for low-achieving students and for second language learners in content-area classes (Readence, Bean, & Baldwin, 2001).

How could it be used in mathematics instruction?

Much of the vocabulary of mathematics can be represented visually. This strategy may be used by students as they are introduced to new vocabulary to make immediate visual associations. As students discover the critical characteristics of a concept or make personal associations, they can put these together with the definitions and visuals to deepen their understanding of the concept.

How to us it:

1. Select vocabulary terms that would be appropriate for using VVWA.

2. Direct students to draw a rectangle divided into four sections for each term.

3. Instruct students to write the vocabulary word in the upper-left box of the rectangle. Instruct them to write the text definition of the term or give them a definition to write in the lower-left box.

4. Direct students to draw a visual representation of the vocabulary word (perhaps found in a graphic in the text) in the upper-right box of the rectangle. Then suggest that they make their own personal association, an example or characteristic, to put in the fourth box at the lower right.

Vocabulary Term	Visual Representation
Definition	Personal Association or Characteristic

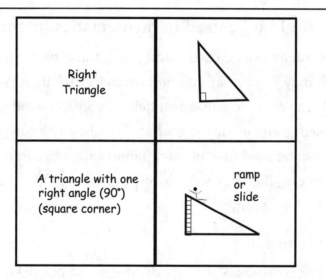

Right Triangle	
A triangle with one right angle (90°) (square corner)	ramp or slide

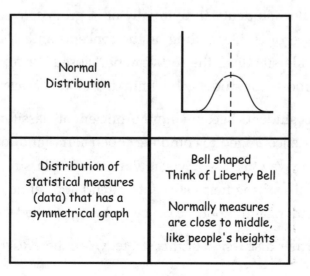

Normal Distribution	
Distribution of statistical measures (data) that has a symmetrical graph	Bell shaped Think of Liberty Bell Normally measures are close to middle, like people's heights

M-9. Word Sort

What is it?

Word sorts (Gillett & Temple, 1983) help students recognize the semantic relationships among key concepts printed on 3" x 5" cards. This strategy can be used in two different ways. In a "closed sort," the teacher provides categories into which students assign the words. In an "open sort," students group words into categories and create their own labels for each category. Word sorts help students develop a deeper understanding of key concepts. They also can be used to develop the complex reasoning skills of classification and deduction.

How could it be used in mathematics instruction?

This strategy can be used throughout a unit by creating a "word wall," which may be used at different times in various ways. Sorting the words can serve to engage students in both activating prior knowledge and evaluating what they already know about the terms. Sorts can be used to explore different categories into which the terms may be classified or can be incorporated to help students explain their understanding.

How to use it:

1. List terms on 3" x 5" cards (one word per card).

2. Allow students, individually or in groups, to sort the words into categories. Depending on the concepts and students' level of understanding, the sorts can be "closed" or "open." Model this process for students by "thinking aloud" as cards are sorted.

3. As students become more proficient at classifying, they should be encouraged to complete "open sorts" and to find more than one way to classify vocabulary terms. Classifying and then reclassifying helps students extend and refine their understanding of the concepts being studied.

For further discussion of this strategy, see the *TRCA Teacher's Manual*, p. 89.

Vocabulary Development

Geometry Word Sort

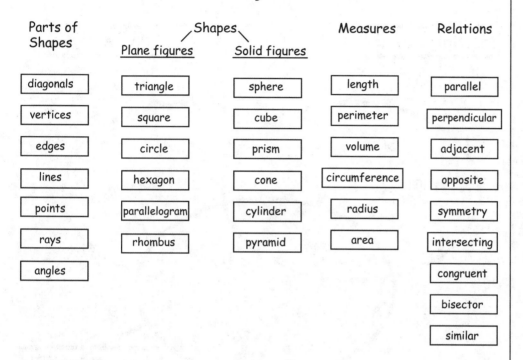

Parts of Shapes	Shapes		Measures	Relations
	Plane figures	Solid figures		
diagonals	triangle	sphere	length	parallel
vertices	square	cube	perimeter	perpendicular
edges	circle	prism	volume	adjacent
lines	hexagon	cone	circumference	opposite
points	parallelogram	cylinder	radius	symmetry
rays	rhombus	pyramid	area	intersecting
angles				congruent
				bisector
				similar

A variation of a word sort is to provide sets of four or five terms. In each set, three of the four terms (or four of the five terms) are related in some way. The student explains the relationship and identifies one term that is unrelated to the others. For example, each list of terms below has one unrelated term once a relationship among the other terms is identified.

length	cubic	acute	similar
perimeter	linear	prime	reflection
volume	quadratic	scalene	rotation
radius	variable	equilateral	translation
width		right	

Vocabulary Development

Number Sort (a variation on Word Sort)

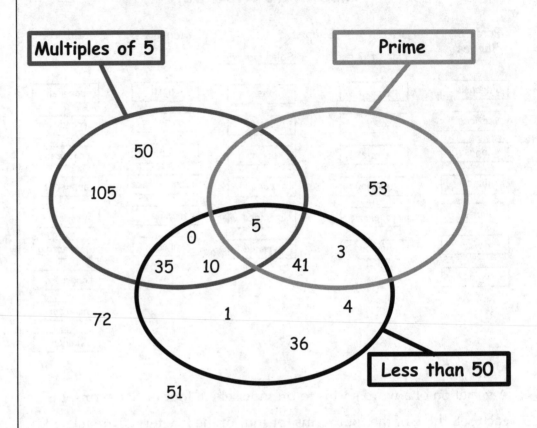

This graphic example could be an exercise if students are asked to place the numbers correctly in the picture.

Vocabulary Development

Symbols are part of the vocabulary of mathematics. The next three strategies are actually games, but these games have a vocabulary development feature with respect to symbols. Such games may help students learn and recall mathematics symbols. They can be adapted for use with other topics.

M-10. Concentration

What is it?

Adapted from the format of the TV game show, the concentration strategy helps students review concepts they have learned. Metric concentration, a variation from a strategy developed by the National Education Association, is an example of how mathematics teachers can help students store what they have learned about metric equivalents. The components of the game include not only pairs that match but also distracting pairs. Consequently, the game goes beyond asking players to rely on memory alone. To win, students must think about metric principles.

How could it be used in mathematics instruction?

This game could be incorporated into a mathematics classroom as a novel way to review and practice with symbol vocabulary. The game requires students to use memory and reasoning.

How to use it:

1. Create a deck of cards of paired metric equivalents (e.g., 120 m and 0.12 km) and distractors (e.g., 120 cm and 12 m).

2. Shuffle the deck and place the cards face down. (See the sample deck illustration on page 90.)

3. Ask one student, or player, to turn over two cards. If the student identifies cards that are equivalent, allow the player to

Vocabulary Development

keep those cards and take another turn. If the cards are not equivalent, the player should turn them face down again and relinquish his or her turn.

4. Players alternate turns until all of the cards except the distractors are gone. The winner is the student with the most pairs of cards.

Sample Deck for Metric Concentration

8.5 m	29 cm	150 mm	0.4 km	0.7 m
70 mm	1.5 km	370 dm	96 cm	96 mm
15 cm	4 m	7 cm	29 m	0.96 dm
400 cm	85 cm	3.7 m	37 m	400 m
0.029 km	8.7 dm	0.85 km	3.7 km	370 cm
3700 m	8500 mm	0.29 m	0.96 m	1500 m

Vocabulary Development

Interactive
Reflective

M-11. Cue Cards

What is it?

In this game, students match mathematics expressions to the verbal language used to read them. The game, as presented by A. Susan Gay of the University of Kansas, is for algebraic expressions but could be modified for other kinds of mathematics expressions.

How could it be used in mathematics instruction?

This activity could be used in a mathematics class as a review or as a novel way to practice with symbol vocabulary. As students hear the expressions read aloud, they construct meaning and validate their understanding of symbols.

How to use it:

1. Provide each student (or pairs of students) with a set of six to eight cards. Each card should have a mathematics statement given in symbols. (See the example set of cards on page 92.)

2. Prepare cue cards with phrases to read for the mathematics statement. You may have more than one cue card corresponding to one statement; that is, there may be different (equivalent) phrases for one mathematics statement given in symbols.

3. Display and read the cue cards aloud one at a time. As each phrase is presented, ask students to select and hold up a matching response (one of the mathematics statements) card. Visually check for correct responses.

Vocabulary Development

Set of cards for each student:

$n + 7$	$7 - n$	$n/7$	$7/n$
$n - 7$	$7n$	$n > 7$	$n < 7$

Cue cards:

A number n is less than 7	7 more than a number n
A number n decreased by 7	The sum of a number n and 7
7 is less than a number n	The difference between n and 7
7 divided by a number n	The quotient of a number n and 7
7 subtracted from a number n	7 less than a number n
The product of a number n and 7	A number n increased by 7
7 times a number n	7 is greater than a number n

Vocabulary Development

M-12. Number Cubes

What is it?

The goal of number cubes is for players to order pairs of fractions or decimals. To achieve this goal, the players must decode and comprehend mathematics symbols, compare their values, and then justify the relationship between them.

How could it be used in mathematics instruction?

This game can be used to review or to provide a novel way to practice with the symbol vocabulary of fractions and decimals. The game requires students to use concepts of ordering fractions or decimals and to verbalize their reasoning for an order.

How to use it:

1. Construct a pair of cubes with fractions or decimals on each face. For example:

Cube A	Cube B	Cube A	Cube B
$\frac{1}{2}$	$\frac{3}{8}$	0.3	0.49
$\frac{2}{3}$	$\frac{1}{3}$	0.04	0.5
$\frac{4}{7}$	$\frac{5}{6}$	0.055	0.07
$\frac{1}{5}$	$\frac{3}{5}$	0.91	0.061
$\frac{3}{4}$	$\frac{1}{4}$	0.709	0.706
$\frac{7}{8}$	$\frac{2}{7}$	0.09	0.88

2. Explain to players that the goal of the game is to earn points by rolling cubes and correctly identifying which cube shows the greater value. A correct response earns a player two points. The first player to reach the score of 30 (or some predetermined score) wins the game.

Vocabulary Development

3. Begin play by letting players roll a cube to determine the order of play.

4. The first player then rolls the cubes, identifies which cube shows the larger value, and explains the answer. The discussion after each play of correct and incorrect answers ensures that players do not win by guessing and also helps reinforce understanding. Play rotates until there is a winner.

Informational Text

M-13. Anticipation/Prediction Guide

What is it?

Anticipation/prediction guides (Herber, 1978) are a set of carefully selected statements that serve as a pre/post inventory for a reading selection. They are designed to activate and assess students' prior knowledge, to focus reading, and to motivate reluctant readers by stimulating their interest in the topic. Because the statements are selected to focus on important concepts in the reading, students should be prepared to focus on and pay attention to this information. Students should read closely in order to get evidence that supports or answers their predictions.

How could it be used in mathematics instruction?

When introduced as a pre-reading activity, these guides help students focus on and pay attention to critical information. They also may help students become more actively involved as they search for supporting information and for answers to their own questions. Teachers may find anticipation guides useful in identifying students' misconceptions and thus adapt their instruction to correct these.

How to use it:

1. Identify concepts you want students to learn from reading.

2. Create four to six statements that support or challenge students' beliefs and experiences (e.g., important points, major concepts, contentious ideas, or misconceptions) about the topic.

3. Prior to reading, students (individually or as a group) react to each statement, formulate a response (under the "me" column), and prepare to defend their opinions.

4. Ask students to explain their responses to each statement.

5. Ask students to read the selection to find evidence that supports or disconfirms each statement ("text" column). Students may be encouraged to rewrite any false statement in a way that makes it true.

M𝒸REL

Informational Text

6. Lead a discussion about what students learned from their reading.

For further discussion of this strategy, see the *TRCA Teacher's Manual*, pp. 104–106.

Anticipation Guide
Multiples and Divisors

Directions: In the column labeled *Me*, place a check next to any statement with which you agree. After reading the text, compare your opinions about those statements with information in the text.

Me	Text	
_____	_____	1. Multiples relate to multiplying and divisors relate to dividing.
_____	_____	2. 0 is a multiple of any number.
_____	_____	3. 0 is a divisor of any number.
_____	_____	4. Multiples of 2 are called even numbers.
_____	_____	5. Multiples of 1 are called odd numbers.
_____	_____	6. Every number is a multiple of itself.
_____	_____	7. Every number is a divisor of itself.

Note: Basic format only from *Teaching Reading in Content Areas*, by H. Herber, 1978, Englewood Cliffs, NJ: Prentice Hall. Copyright 1978 by Prentice Hall.

Anticipation Guide
Integers

Directions: In the column labeled *Me*, place a check next to any statement with which you agree. After reading the text, compare your opinions about those statements with information in the text.

Me   Text

_____   _____   1. The sum of two integers is always greater than both of the numbers being added.

_____   _____   2. It is possible to add two integers and get a sum less than zero.

_____   _____   3. The sum of zero and any other integer is always the other integer.

_____   _____   4. The product of two integers is always greater than both of the numbers being multiplied.

_____   _____   5. The product of two positive integers is always positive.

_____   _____   6. The product of two negative integers is always negative.

Note: Basic format only from *Teaching Reading in Content Areas*, by H. Herber, 1978, Englewood Cliffs, NJ: Prentice Hall. Copyright 1978 by Prentice Hall.

Anticipation Guide
Statistics

Directions: In the column labeled *Me*, place a check next to any statement with which you agree. After reading the text, compare your opinions about those statements with information in the text.

Me   Text

_____   _____   1. There are several kinds of averages for a set of data.

_____   _____   2. The mode is the middle number in a set of data.

_____   _____   3. Range tells how far apart numbers are in a set of data.

_____   _____   4. Outliers are always ignored.

_____   _____   5. Averages are always given as percents.

Note: Basic format only from *Teaching Reading in Content Areas*, by H. Herber, 1978, Englewood Cliffs, NJ: Prentice Hall. Copyright 1978 by Prentice Hall.

M-14. Five-Step Problem Solving

What is it?

Braselton and Decker (1994) assert that students' comprehension of word problems can be enhanced by teaching them to read word problems as meaningful passages — as short stories from which students can construct meaning based on their prior knowledge and experience. Teachers use this strategy by presenting students with a graphic organizer that leads them through a five-step problem-solving process (similar to Polya's four-step process): restate the problem/question; determine what information is needed to solve the problem; plan the steps (calculations) to be performed; carry out the plan (perform the calculations); and evaluate the reasonableness of the solution.

How could it be used in mathematics instruction?

This strategy gives students a graphic organizer to use in the problem-solving process. It can help students understand the steps and explain their reasoning throughout the process.

How to use it:

1. Introduce students to the layout and design of the graphic organizer (page 100). Point out that the diamond shape of the graphic reinforces the fact that all students begin with the same information about a problem and should arrive at the same conclusion, if they are successful at solving the problem. Between the top and bottom point of the diamond, students may use a variety of problem-solving strategies, depending upon their reasoning and experience.

2. Explain each of the steps outlined in the graphic.

3. Present students with a word problem, reading it aloud and asking students about their prior knowledge of the situation and elements included in the "story."

4. Model for students how to complete the first step of the organizer, restating the question in a number of ways. Ask students to identify which version is the clearest and to explain the reasoning behind their choice. Once students know how to approach the problem, they will feel more confident about solving it.

5. Model how to complete the remaining steps in the graphic organizer.

6. When students understand the steps in the graphic organizer, offer them opportunities for guided practice. Select another word problem, and lead them through each step of the process. Ask students to discuss their thinking as they read the problem and to articulate the reasons for the responses they give. Encourage divergent thinking. Point out to students that there may be several different approaches to the same problem.

7. Let students work in small groups to discuss and complete several more problems using the five-step graphic organizer.

8. Allot a few minutes over the next several days for students to practice solving word problems using the organizer. Point out that the graphic organizer is a guide, not a set formula for solving problems. Students should see that several approaches to the same problem can still result in the same solution.

Graphic Organizer for Five-Step Problem Solving

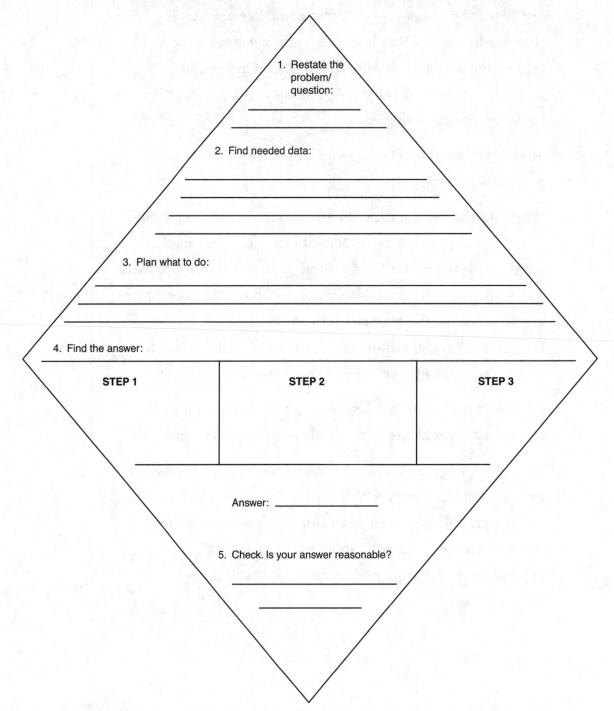

McREL

Informational Text

M-15. Graphic Organizer

What is it?

Graphic organizers include things like webs, maps, charts, and diagrams. They provide a visual representation of key concepts and related terms, helping students see relationships among ideas and show how ideas link together. They are effective tools for thinking, note taking, and learning. They help students represent abstract ideas in more concrete forms, depict relationships among facts and concepts, organize ideas, and store or recall information. Graphic organizers can be used to depict various aspects or elements of a concept and the relationships among them.

How could it be used in mathematics instruction?

This strategy can be incorporated throughout a lesson or unit. It can be used to engage students by having them share what they know about a topic. Graphic organizers can help students make connections, explain relationships, and elaborate on what they have learned. Throughout a lesson or unit, a teacher can use student-constructed organizers to evaluate students' understanding and check for misconceptions.

How to use it:

1. Explain the purpose and benefits of using graphic organizers.

2. Introduce a specific form of graphic organizer.

3. Model how to use the selected organizer.

4. Provide multiple opportunities for students to practice using graphic organizers.

5. Encourage students to construct their own organizers.

For further discussion of this strategy, see the *TRCA Teacher's Manual*, pp. 109–111, 134, and 135.

MCREL

Notes

Informational Text

Concept Definition Webs

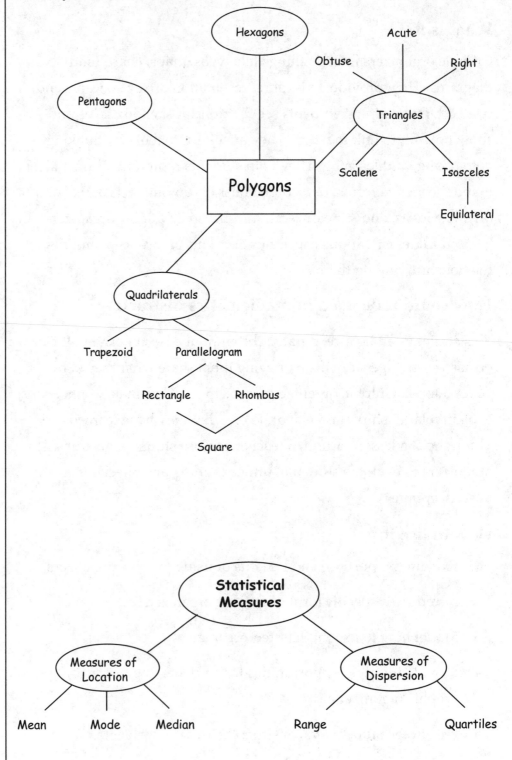

Informational Text

Generalization/Principle Diagram

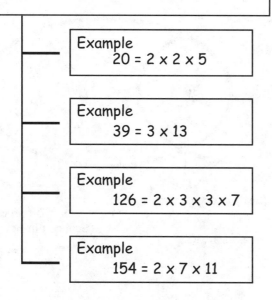

Generalization or Principle
Every composite number can be
written as a product of prime numbers.

Example
20 = 2 x 2 x 5

Example
39 = 3 x 13

Example
126 = 2 x 3 x 3 x 7

Example
154 = 2 x 7 x 11

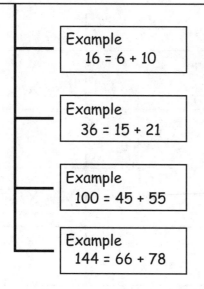

Generalization or Principle
Every square number can be written
as the sum of two triangular numbers.

Example
16 = 6 + 10

Example
36 = 15 + 21

Example
100 = 45 + 55

Example
144 = 66 + 78

Informational Text

Compare/Contrast Organizers

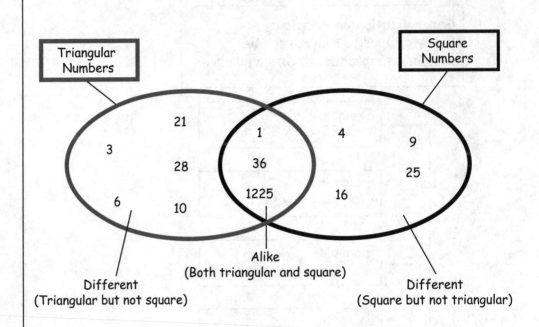

	Pyramids	Prisms
3-dimensional solid	X	X
One base	X	
Pair of parallel bases		X
All triangular faces except base	X	
Polyhedron	X	X
Cube		X

Informational Text

The following are other graphic organizers commonly used in mathematics.

Factor trees

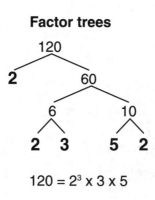

$$120 = 2^3 \times 3 \times 5$$

Multiplication Table

×	1	2	3	4	5	6	7	8	9	10
1	1	2	3	4	5	6	7	8	9	10
2	2	4	6	8	10	12	14	16	18	20
3	3	6	9	12	15	18	21	24	27	30
4	4	8	12	16	20	24	28	32	36	40
5	5	10	15	20	25	30	35	40	45	50
6	6	12	18	24	30	36	42	48	54	60
7	7	14	21	28	35	42	49	56	63	70
8	8	16	24	32	40	48	56	64	72	80
9	9	18	27	36	45	54	63	72	81	90
10	10	20	30	40	50	60	70	80	90	100

The following list and diagram are examples of graphic organizers for solving the problem of counting the number of possible sundaes given three choices of ice creams, two choices of syrups, and two choices of toppings.

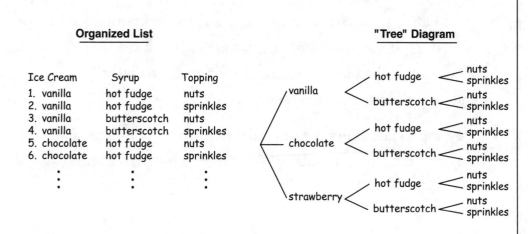

Organized List

Ice Cream	Syrup	Topping
1. vanilla	hot fudge	nuts
2. vanilla	hot fudge	sprinkles
3. vanilla	butterscotch	nuts
4. vanilla	butterscotch	sprinkles
5. chocolate	hot fudge	nuts
6. chocolate	hot fudge	sprinkles

"Tree" Diagram

Informational Text

M-16. Group Summarizing

What is it?

Group or class summaries help learners review and remember information. Summarizing information requires readers to distinguish between key concepts and subordinate ideas. It also requires the ability to condense information (Brown, Day, & Jones, 1983). Summarizing is a sophisticated skill; therefore, modeling is critical.

How could it be used in mathematics instruction?

This strategy is helpful when you want students to explain what they have learned through a summary. The strategy models for students a way to organize information for a report about what they have learned.

How to use it:

1. Instruct students to survey the text selection to identify major topics to focus on while reading.

2. Next, divide the chalkboard or chart paper into parts, and label the sections based on major topics. These sections provide students with a purpose for reading.

3. After students have read the text, ask for volunteers to provide information for each major topic and record the information in sentence form on the board or chart paper. Class discussion is a key part of the process. Students need to decide what information is critical and how to state it clearly.

4. Develop a class summary of critical information, and transfer this information to the labeled sections of the chart.

5. To help students learn to identify major topics, modify this strategy by recording student information first. Ask students to identify major topics and then organize the information into identified topics.

For further discussion of this strategy, see the *TRCA Teacher's Manual*, pp. 112–113

Sample Organizational Format for Group Summarizing Activity

Pascal's Triangle	
Description $$\begin{array}{ccccccccccccc} & & & & & & 1 & & & & & & \\ & & & & & 1 & & 1 & & & & & \\ & & & & 1 & & 2 & & 1 & & & & \\ & & & 1 & & 3 & & 3 & & 1 & & & \\ & & 1 & & 4 & & 6 & & 4 & & 1 & & \\ & 1 & & 5 & & 10 & & 10 & & 5 & & 1 & \\ 1 & & 6 & & 15 & & 20 & & 15 & & 6 & & 1 \end{array}$$ Each number is entered in the triangular array by adding the two numbers above it.	**Patterns** — symmetry — sum of any row is a power of 2 — diagonals: 1's, counting numbers, triangular numbers
Uses — combinatorial patterns — binomial coefficients	**Interesting Facts** This arithmetic triangle was known to the Chinese as early as 1100 A.D. Italian mathematicians investigated properties of the triangle in 1550. Pascal identified it in 1650.

Note: Basic format only from "Content Reading Instruction in the Primary Grades: Perceptions and Strategies," by M. W. Olson and T. C. Gee, 1991, *The Reading Teacher*, *45*(4), pp. 298–307. Copyright 1991 by the International Reading Association.

M-17. Knowledge Rating Chart

What is it?

Davis and Gerber (1994) suggest that mathematics teachers can assess students' prior knowledge by using a knowledge rating. This strategy differs from the anticipation/prediction guide in that students rate their working knowledge of the concepts to be covered in the lesson. Teachers can use the information students provide to inform instruction.

How could it be used in mathematics instruction?

This strategy allows students to activate prior knowledge by previewing a topic. It also helps them focus on some important concepts to learn about while studying the topic. Teachers can adapt instruction based on students' prior knowledge.

How to use it:

1. Present students with a list of the major concepts to be covered in the unit, chapter, or lesson.

2. Ask students to rate how familiar they are with these terms.

Sample Knowledge Rating Chart.

Directions: Rate the following statistics terms as follows:

1. I've never heard of the word before.
2. I've heard the term, but I don't know how it applies to mathematics.
3. I understand the meaning of this term and can apply it to a mathematics problem.

mean _____   line of best fit_____

median _____   correlation_____

mode _____   range_____

weighted average _____

      normal distribution _____

      bimodal distribution _____

      skewed distribution _____

      flat distribution _____

M-18. What I Know; Want to Learn; Learned (K-W-L)

What is it?

Another strategy that helps students predict and connect new information with prior knowledge is K-W-L (Ogle, 1986, 1989). K-W-L can be used to brainstorm prior knowledge, to preview vocabulary and/or concepts, and to help students recall what they have read.

How could it be used in mathematics instruction?

This strategy can engage students in further exploration of a topic through reading. Its use could follow an investigation that has given students prior knowledge, providing students with an opportunity to explain what they already know and what they still need or want to learn. It gives them a chance to elaborate on what they have learned and expect to learn through their reading. It also provides teachers with the opportunity to evaluate students' understanding and check for misconceptions.

How to use it:

1. Introduce students to the strategy in conjunction with a new topic or text selection.

2. Provide students with a K-W-L chart, and instruct them to fill out the first two sections of the chart. Students' misconceptions generally show up in the "K" column.

3. Ask students to read the text selection purposefully to discover answers for the questions they or other class members posed.

4. Ask students to identify what they have learned. Then ask them to record answers to their questions as well as any other important information they have learned. Let students make changes to the "K" column when their prior knowledge was inaccurate.

For further discussion of this strategy, including variations, see the *TRCA Teacher's Manual*, pp. 116–118.

Informational Text

K-W-L Worksheet

K What I know	W What I want to find out	L What I learned

Note: Basic format only from "The K-W-L: A Teaching Model That Develops Active Reading of Expository Text," by D. Ogle, 1986, *The Reading Teacher*, 39, 564–570.

K-W-L Fibonacci's Sequence

K What I know	W What I want to find out	L What I learned
Fibonacci's Sequence 1, 1, 2, 3, 5, 8, 13, 21 ... Fibonacci's Rabbits Multiplying populations	How do bees fit in the Fibonacci pattern? What is the connection between the Fibonacci sequence and the Golden ratio? Is there a formula for the Fibonacci number sequence? What do pineapples and pinecones have to do with Fibonacci?	

Note: Basic format only from "The K-W-L: A Teaching Model That Develops Active Reading of Expository Text," by D. Ogle, 1986, *The Reading Teacher*, 39, 564–570.

Informational Text

K-W-L Prime Numbers

K What I know	W What I want to find out	L What I learned

A prime number has exactly two divisors (factors), 1 and itself.
 	
2 is the only even prime number.
 	
Successive odd numbers that are both primes are twin primes:
   3 and 5
   5 and 7
   11 and 13
	Why are prime numbers so important?
	
	What is the sieve of Eratosthenes, and how do you use it to get primes?
	
	Is there a connection between prime numbers and perfect numbers?
	
	What is an emirp?
	
	What are some patterns related to prime numbers?	

Note: Basic format only from "The K-W-L: A Teaching Model That Develops Active Reading of Expository Text," by D. Ogle, 1986, *The Reading Teacher*, 39, 564–570.

K-W-L Tessellations

K What I know	W What I want to find out	L What I learned
What a tesselation is Squares, equilateral triangles, regular hexagons can be used for a tesselation. You cannot use a regular pentagon for a tesselation.	What combination of shapes can be used in a tesselation? What is meant by a code for a tesselation? What are some irregular shapes that tesselate?	

Note: Basic format only from "The K-W-L: A Teaching Model That Develops Active Reading of Expository Text," by D. Ogle, 1986, *The Reading Teacher*, 39, 564–570.

M-19. K-N-W-S (K-W-L for Word Problems)

What is it?

In this strategy students use a worksheet similar to K-W-L to analyze and plan how to approach solving a word problem. Using the word problem, students answer what facts they KNOW, what information is NOT relevant, WHAT the problem asks them to find, and what STRATEGY they can use to solve the problem.

How could it be used in mathematics instruction?

This strategy can engage students in exploration of word problems as they decode the given information, determine the question, and select an appropriate solution method. It can provide teachers with the opportunity to evaluate students' understanding and check for misconceptions.

How to use it:

1. Introduce students to the four-column K-N-W-S worksheet.

2. Present students with a word problem, and model how to fill in information in each of the columns. Explain how you knew what information should be included in each column; teachers often show "how" but don't explain "how you know."

3. Ask students to work in groups to complete K-N-W-S worksheets for other word problems. Ask students to discuss with their groups how they knew what to put in the columns.

4. Give students ongoing independent practice using this strategy to solve word problems. Periodically ask students to write an explanation of their reasoning process.

Informational Text

K-N-W-S Worksheet

K What facts do I KNOW from the information in the problem?	N Which information do I NOT need?	W WHAT does the problem ask me to find?	S What STRATEGY/ operation/tools will I use to solve the problem?

Problem: The ends of a rope are tied to two trees, 500 feet apart. Every 10 feet an 8-foot post is set 2 feet into the ground to support the rope. How many support posts are needed?

K What facts do I KNOW from the information in the problem?	N Which information do I NOT need?	W WHAT does the problem ask me to find?	S What STRATEGY/ operation/tools will I use to solve the problem?
Trees are 500 feet apart. Posts are placed at 10-foot intervals between the trees.	The posts are 8 feet tall. The posts are set 2 feet into the ground.	How many support posts are needed?	Draw a model to understand how to place posts. Solve the problem with the trees closer and find a pattern. There are 50 (500 ÷ 10) 10-foot intervals between the trees.

Informational Text

M-20. Pairs Read

What is it?

Pairs read is a strategy that requires collaborative learning. Students help each other increase their knowledge and understanding of the text by reading the text aloud to each other. While one student reads aloud, another student listens and then summarizes the main ideas.

How could it be used in mathematics instruction?

This strategy allows students to use both listening and reading skills to learn new information. Students must explain what they understand about what they heard or read and ask clarifying questions. Because students share what they have learned about a topic with other students, they actively participate in interpreting mathematics content.

How to use it:

1. Select a passage for students to read.

2. Arrange students into pairs; ask one to be the coach and the other to be the reader.

3. Ask the reader to read the first paragraph or section of text aloud to the coach.

4. Then ask the coach to summarize the main idea and supporting details. The coach can ask the reader questions to help clarify the reading.

5. Instruct students to reverse roles, and ask the new reader to read the next paragraph or section of text.

6. Ask the new coach to summarize what was read.

7. Instruct students to continue alternating roles until they have completed the passage.

8. Once the entire passage has been read, ask students to summarize the main idea and discuss the supporting details.

For further discussion of this strategy, including variations, see the *TRCA Teacher's Manual,* pp. 119–120.

Informational Text

Preactive

M-21. Prereading Plan

What is it?

The prereading plan (Langer, 1981) provides a framework for activating and extending prior knowledge.

How could it be used in mathematics instruction?

This strategy can be used to engage students in thinking about a topic prior to reading about it. By generating interest and activating prior knowledge, the plan can serve to make students more attentive in reading, to focus them on associations or connections, and to help them monitor comprehension.

How to use it?

1. Identify the central concept in the selection and introduce it to students by asking, "What comes to your mind when you hear the word (or phrase) _____?" (e.g., *Fractals*)

2. Suggest that students individually write down all of their associations, and then on the chalkboard make a composite list of all the different responses (e.g., "fractions," "something in nature," "geometry," "patterns").

3. Let students reflect on why each association was made by asking, "What made you think of _____?" (e.g., "The word *fractals* sounds like *fractions*." "A picture I saw looked like a lot of triangles, and it was called a fractal.")

4. Conclude the activity by saying, "As a result of our discussion, can you think of any other information that you know about this topic?" (e.g., "There might be some connection between fractals and describing things in nature.")

For further discussion of this strategy, see the *TRCA Teacher's Manual*, p. 121.

Notes

Informational Text

Preactive
Reflective

M-22. Problematic Situation

What is it?

Problematic situation is a strategy that activates what students already know about a topic, motivates students to want to read the text, and helps them to focus on the main ideas presented in the text as they read. Developed by Vacca and Vacca (1993), it can be used with any text material dealing with a problem/solution relationship.

How could it be used in mathematics instruction?

This strategy can be used to engage students in mathematics problems that lead them to want to explore ideas through reading. It can also be used to evaluate students' understanding of the mathematics content in a problem situation. This strategy is an effective way to bring real problem-solving contexts into mathematics.

How to use it:

1. Design a problematic situation similar to one presented in a selected text passage. Provide enough relevant information about the situation so students will be able to focus their attention on key ideas in the passage. Be sure to define clearly the context of the problem.

2. Pose the problem to students. Let cooperative groups generate and record possible results or solutions. When they have listed their solutions, let them discuss why each one is a good solution or why it would succeed.

3. Ask students to "test" their solutions when they read the assigned text material. Each group should refine or modify their solutions as they gain new information from their reading.

4. As a final activity, discuss with the class whether some of the students' solutions might be better than those presented by the author.

For further discussion of this strategy, see the *TRCA Teacher's Manual*, pp. 122–123.

116

Informational Text

Examples of Problematic Situations Involving Measurements and Percents

Copy Machine

The copy machine in Ms. Graber's office has a zoom that allows the user to set the machine so that copies will be enlarged or reduced from the original image. The settings for this zoom feature are in percents. The office staff are in the habit of using the zoom feature simply by trying a number of settings until they find the one that fits their needs. But this results in a lot of wasted copies and discarded paper. Ms. Graber would like to give explicit directions to the staff so that they will learn how to set the zoom feature accurately the first time. How would you advise Ms. Graber to write these directions?

Package Design

Your firm has been selected to design a new package for the STARBAR Candy Company. The company is planning to reduce by 10% the size of the current candy bar it sells. The dimensions of the current unwrapped candy bar are 6 inches by 2 inches by 1 inch. The company must reduce the size to cut costs, but management recognizes that reducing the size may affect sales. Your task is to design the packaging so that it will minimize the appearance of the reduction in size. Write your response in the form of a proposal to the chairman of the board of STARBAR Candy Company.

Informational Text

M-23. Reciprocal Teaching

What is it?

Reciprocal teaching (Palincsar & Brown, 1985) is a strategy in which students learn the skills of summarizing, questioning, clarifying, and predicting well enough to perform as an instructor of content. When students become adept at these four skills, they not only instruct one another but also learn metacomprehension (strategic processing) skills they can use while reading independently.

How could it be used in mathematics instruction?

Reciprocal teaching provides students with opportunities to examine mathematics text and to explain to other students how to read and comprehend mathematics material.

How to use it:

1. Explain to students the concept of reciprocal teaching — that we learn best by teaching others.

2. Instruct students in the four skills that they will use to improve their own reading comprehension as well as their classmates' (summarizing, questioning, clarifying, and predicting).

3. While reading a text selection, model for students how to summarize, generate questions, clarify confusing text, and predict. Give students time to practice these skills.

4. Begin to shift some of the responsibility for directing class discussions to the students. Allow them to summarize, generate questions, clarify confusing text, and predict for the class.

5. As students become more proficient, let them take turns leading discussions of text selections.

For further discussion of this strategy, see the *TRCA Teacher's Manual*, pp. 128–129.

Informational Text *Interactive*

M-24. Search Strategy

What is it?

The search strategy can be used when students are asked to research a topic. The project might focus on questions to be answered rather than on a general topic. This comprehensive strategy stimulates students to find answers to questions they generate themselves and they have from their reading.

How could it be used in mathematics instruction?

This strategy is particularly useful when students are extending their knowledge of a mathematics topic by doing further research or investigation.

How to use it:

1. **Select** a specific topic of interest to study.

2. **Establish** what students know, think they know, and want to know about the topic. Write the three categories on the board, and let students work individually first, and then in small groups, to stimulate ideas. Record ideas in all three categories. Encourage participation from all students and develop their confidence by suggesting they know more than they realize.

3. **Ask** any questions to raise curiosity and to challenge students by asking for more specific information when they share their ideas about the topic.

4. **Read** resource material to verify what they know and think they know, to answer questions, and to raise new questions.

5. **Come** together like scholars; share and review responses in small groups.

6. **Hold** a large-group discussion to share learnings and to identify unanswered questions as well as new questions for further research.

For further discussion of this strategy, see the *TRCA Teacher's Manual*, pp. 132–133.

McREL

Informational Text

S	Figurative Numbers
E	<u>Know</u> <u>Think</u> <u>Want to Know</u> square & triangular patterns & uses
A	Are other kinds of figurative numbers useful? How would hexagonal or pentagonal numbers be defined?
R	Research the answers to these questions. Use the text and, if appropriate, other resource material.
C	Share what was learned in groups.
H	Discuss what was learned. Ask new questions.

Informational Text

M-25. Semantic Mapping

What is it?

Semantic mapping (Johnson & Pearson, 1984) is a strategy used to identify relationships among key concepts and related technical terms in a text passage. As such, it works well as an introduction to a topic and to vocabulary that students may encounter during reading. It can be used as a review strategy in which students not only map key concepts but also indicate hierarchies that exist among concepts and related technical terms.

How could it be used in mathematics instruction?

This strategy is useful in reviewing what students know about a topic before learning new ideas. It should help students organize the information they have, make connections, and incorporate new ideas into their information.

How to use it:

1. Model for students how to perform this strategy:

    Write on the board a key concept from the unit you have just completed. List a number of related concepts and technical terms. (These may come from the text or simply be part of your general knowledge base about the topic.) As you create this list, explain your thought process: why the key concept made you think of each term you listed, and the connections you see between each term and the key concept. Next, create a web or map for the terms you have listed. In order to do that, you will need to classify, or group, these terms into categories. Verbalize your thoughts as you identify appropriate categories, label each, and write the terms under the appropriate category label.

2. When students understand the semantic mapping strategy, write on the board a key concept from the lesson you are about to teach. Let students collaborate in small groups to brainstorm as

many related words and concepts as they can think of. Ask them to help the student recorder classify the words into groups.

3. Ask the small groups to share the semantic maps they created so that one large semantic map can be created on the board. Add any missing words that students will need to know to understand the passage.

4. After students finish reading the text passage, ask them to add new information they learned. Using a different color chalk will highlight which terms are a product of new learning.

For further discussion of this strategy, see the *TRCA Teacher's Manual*, pp. 134–135.

Semantic Map

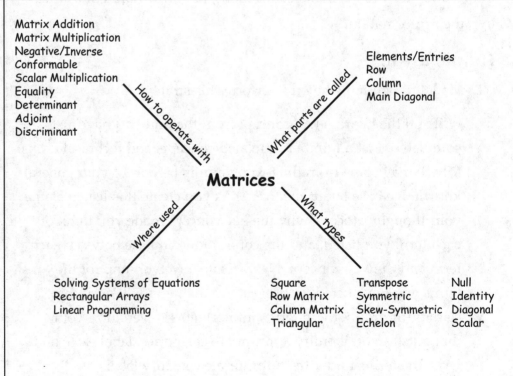

Matrix Addition
Matrix Multiplication
Negative/Inverse
Conformable
Scalar Multiplication
Equality
Determinant
Adjoint
Discriminant

How to operate with

What parts are called

Elements/Entries
Row
Column
Main Diagonal

Matrices

Where used

What types

Solving Systems of Equations
Rectangular Arrays
Linear Programming

Square
Row Matrix
Column Matrix
Triangular

Transpose
Symmetric
Skew-Symmetric
Echelon

Null
Identity
Diagonal
Scalar

Informational Text

M-26. Survey, Question, Read, Recite, Review (SQ3R)

What is it?

SQ3R (Robinson, 1961) is a versatile study strategy because it engages students during each phase of the reading process. Students preview the text material to develop predictions and to set a purpose for reading by generating questions about the topic; they read actively, searching for answers to those questions; they monitor their comprehension as they summarize; and they evaluate their comprehension through review activities.

How could it be used in mathematics instruction?

This strategy provides students with a structured way to preview and read as they explore text material. As discussed in the Text Style section of this supplement, studying mathematics text can be especially challenging. A deliberate study strategy such as SQ3R can help students focus and read actively.

How to use it:

Provide students with the following instructions. Model how to respond to each set of questions or tasks. Assign text passages for students to read and practice the strategy.

1. Survey what you are about to read.

   • Think about the title: What do I know about this subject? What do I want to know?

   • Glance over headings, or skim the first sentences of paragraphs.

   • Look at illustrations and graphic aids.

   • Read the first paragraph.

   • Read the last paragraph or summary.

Informational Text

2. Question.

- Turn the title into a question. This becomes the major purpose for your reading.

- Write down any questions that come to mind during the survey.

- Turn headings and subheadings into questions.

- Turn illustrations and graphic aids into questions.

- Determine the meaning of any unfamiliar vocabulary.

3. Read actively.

- Read to search for answers to questions.

- Respond to questions and use context clues for unfamiliar words.

- React to unclear passages, confusing terms, and questionable statements by generating additional questions.

4. Recite.

- Look away from answers in the book to recall what was read.

- Recite answers to questions aloud or write them down.

- Reread text for unanswered questions.

5. Review.

- Answer the major purpose questions.

- Look over answers and all parts of the chapter to organize information.

- Summarize the information learned by creating a graphic organizer that depicts the main ideas, by drawing a flow chart, by writing a summary, by participating in a group discussion, or by writing an explanation of how this material has changed your perceptions.

For further discussion of this strategy, see the *TRCA Teacher's Manual*, pp. 130–131.

Informational Text

M-27. SQRQCQ

What is it?

This study strategy designed by Fay (1965) is modeled after the SQ3R strategy and is intended to assist students in reading and learning mathematics. Its particular use is in reading and solving word problems in mathematics. The strategy involves previewing, setting purpose, and monitoring success.

How could it be used in mathematics instruction?

Students often have difficulty with word problems because of reading difficulties or because they have trouble picking out the relevant information. This strategy can help them focus on a plan to decide what a problem is asking, what information is critical, and what process to use in solving the problem. It also requires students to reflect on the process and the reasonableness of a solution.

How to use it:

Provide students with the following SQRQCQ steps. Model the strategy with a word problem, and then give students time to practice the strategy with other problems.

1. *Survey.* Students read the problem quickly to get an idea or a general understanding of it.

2. *Question.* Students question what information the problem requires, for example, "What is this problem asking for?"

3. *Read.* Students carefully read the problem to identify the relevant information, facts, and details they need to solve it.

4. *Question.* Students question how to solve the problem, for example, "What operations must be performed and in what order?"

5. *Compute (or construct).* Students do the computations or otherwise construct a solution to the problem.

6. *Question.* Students question whether the solution process and answer seem to be correct, for example, "Were the computations performed accurately and is the answer reasonable?"

M-28. Think-Aloud

What is it?

Think-alouds (Davey, 1983) help students understand the kind of thinking required by a specific task. The teacher models a thinking process by verbalizing thoughts while reading, processing information, or performing some learning task. Students see how the teacher attempts to construct meaning for unfamiliar vocabulary, engages in dialogue with the author, or recognizes non-comprehension and selects a strategy to help with comprehension. Struggling readers especially benefit from observing what skilled readers think about while they read.

How could it be used in mathematics instruction?

Think-alouds provide opportunities for teachers to model how to explore mathematics text. This might include previewing a chapter by looking at titles, subtitles, graphic organizers, and pictures to get an overall view of what the chapter is going to be about. It might include making predictions, creating mental pictures, connecting information to prior knowledge, creating analogies, and verbalizing obstacles as well as strategies to overcome these obstacles while reading mathematics material.

How to use it:

1. Explain that reading is an active process that involves thinking and sense making.

2. Select a passage to read aloud that students might find difficult.

3. While students read this passage silently, read it aloud. As you read, verbalize your thoughts, your questions, and the processes you use to solve comprehension problems.

For further discussion of this strategy, see the *TRCA Teacher's Manual*, pp. 139–141.

Sieve of Eratosthenes

> Am I sure about this?

> We could check each one, but there must be an easier way.

We know it is **not possible to find all the prime numbers** but we can **find all prime numbers less than a given number.** One way to do this is to use the **sieve** method, so called because with this method composite numbers drop out leaving only prime numbers. The sieve method was first used by **Eratosthenes of Alexandria (c. 200 BC)** and carried his name.

> I know what a sieve is for cooking. Strange to use it in mathematics.

> This name is hard to pronounce. Maybe I should ask.

> Wow! About 2200 years ago.

To illustrate this method, let us use the whole numbers from 1 to 60 and proceed to find all prime numbers less than 60. List all integers from 1 to 60.

The **number 1 is neither prime nor composite,** so cross it out. The next number 2 is prime, so circle it. The other **even numbers (multiples of 2) are composite,** so cross them out.

> I always have to think about this. Oh, yes! A prime must have two factors, 1 and itself, not just 1.

> Let me check. I guess an even number has 1 and 2 as factors plus itself.

1̶	②	3	4̶	5	6̶	7	8̶	9	1̶0̶
11	1̶2̶	13	1̶4̶	15	1̶6̶	17	1̶8̶	19	2̶0̶
21	2̶2̶	23	2̶4̶	25	2̶6̶	27	2̶8̶	29	3̶0̶
31	3̶2̶	33	3̶4̶	35	3̶6̶	37	3̶8̶	39	4̶0̶
41	4̶2̶	43	4̶4̶	45	4̶6̶	47	4̶8̶	49	5̶0̶
51	5̶2̶	53	5̶4̶	55	5̶6̶	57	5̶8̶	59	6̶0̶

The first uncircled number is 3, and it must be a prime. Circle 3 and cross out all other multiples of 3, which **must be composites.**

> Oh, this must be because they are divisible by 1, 3, and themselves.

1̶	②	③	4̶	5	6̶	7	8̶	9̶	1̶0̶
11	1̶2̶	13	1̶4̶	1̶5̶	1̶6̶	17	18	19	2̶0̶
2̶1̶	2̶2̶	23	2̶4̶	25	2̶6̶	2̶7̶	2̶8̶	29	3̶0̶
31	3̶2̶	3̶3̶	3̶4̶	35	3̶6̶	37	3̶8̶	3̶9̶	4̶0̶
41	4̶2̶	43	4̶4̶	4̶5̶	4̶6̶	47	4̶8̶	49	5̶0̶
5̶1̶	5̶2̶	53	5̶4̶	55	5̶6̶	5̶7̶	5̶8̶	59	6̶0̶

Now, the first uncircled number, 5, must be a prime. Circle 5 and **cross out all other multiples of 5.**

Continue in this way until all numbers have either been circled or crossed out.

> We were crossing out composite numbers. All other multiples of 5 are composite.

1̶	②	③	4̶	⑤	6̶	⑦	8̶	9̶	1̶0̶
⑪	1̶2̶	13	1̶4̶	1̶5̶	1̶6̶	17	18	19	2̶0̶
2̶1̶	2̶2̶	23	2̶4̶	2̶5̶	26	2̶7̶	2̶8̶	29	30
31	3̶2̶	3̶3̶	3̶4̶	3̶5̶	36	37	3̶8̶	3̶9̶	4̶0̶
41	4̶2̶	43	4̶4̶	4̶5̶	4̶6̶	47	4̶8̶	4̶9̶	5̶0̶
5̶1̶	5̶2̶	53	5̶4̶	5̶5̶	5̶6̶	5̶7̶	5̶8̶	59	6̶0̶

> Maybe I should check this. Does this mean I have to check that all the others are prime?

Notice that, in this situation, once we **cross out the multiples of 7, no more numbers get crossed out.** The remaining numbers are all primes. The primes less than 60 are 2, 3, 5, 7, 11, 13, 17, 19, 23, 29, 31, 37, 41, 43, 47, 53, and 59.

M-29. Three-Level Guide

What is it?

Davis and Gerber (1994) recommend a three-level guide to help students analyze and solve word problems. Using a teacher-constructed graphic organizer, students must evaluate facts, concepts, rules, mathematics ideas, and approaches to solving particular word problems.

How could it be used in mathematics instruction?

This strategy can help students focus on the important facts in a word problem. It allows students to check the usefulness of a number of approaches, questions, or computations in solving a problem.

How to use it:

1. Construct a guide for a given problem similar to the one shown on the next page. The first level (Part I) should include a set of facts suggested by the data given in the problem. The students' goal is to analyze each fact to determine if it is true and if it will help them to solve the problem.

2. The second level (Part II) should contain mathematics ideas, rules, or concepts that students can examine to determine which might apply to the problem-solving task.

3. The third level (Part III) should include a list of possible ways to get the answer. Students will analyze these to see which ones might help them solve the problem.

4. Introduce students to the strategy by showing them a problem and the completed three-level guide. Explain what kind of information is included at each level.

5. Model for students how to use the guide in solving the problem.

6. Present students with another problem and guide. Suggest that they analyze the information you have included to determine its validity and usefulness in solving the problem.

Informational Text

7. With advanced students, ask them to select a word problem from the text and complete a three-level guide to be shared with the class.

Three-Level Guide to a Math Problem

Read the problem and then answer each set of questions, following the directions given for the set of questions.

Problem: Sam's Sporting Goods has a markup rate of 40% on Pro tennis rackets. Sam, the store owner, bought 12 Pro tennis rackets for $75 each. Calculate the selling price of a Pro tennis racket at Sam's Sporting Goods.

Part I

Directions: Read the statements. Check Column A if the statement is true according to the problem. Check Column B if the information will help you solve the problem.

A (true?)   B (help?)

_____   _____   Sam's markup rate is 40%.

_____   _____   Sam bought 12 Pro tennis rackets.

_____   _____   Pro tennis rackets are a good buy.

_____   _____   Sam paid $75 for a Pro tennis racket.

_____   _____   The selling price of a Pro tennis racket
                                      is more than $75.

Part II

Directions: Read the statements. Check the ones that contain math ideas useful for this problem. Look at Part I, Column B to check your answer.

_____   Markup equals cost times rate.

_____   Selling price is greater than cost.

_____   Selling price equals cost plus markup.

_____   Markup divided by cost equals markup rate.

_____   A percent of a number is less than the number
                              when the percent is less than 100%.

Part III

Directions: Check the calculations that will help or work in this problem. Look at Parts I and II to check your answers.

_____ $0.4 \times \$75$ _____ $12 \times \$75$

_____ $\$75 \times 40$ _____ $40\% \text{ of } \$75$

_____ $1.4 \times \$75$ _____ $\$75 + (\frac{2}{5} \times \$75)$

Informational Text

M-30. Word Problem Roulette

What is it?

Davis and Gerber (1994) posit that students should discuss and write about the content of word problems. The word problem roulette strategy gives students a chance to collaborate on solving a problem and then to communicate their thought process and solution in writing.

How could it be used in mathematics instruction?

This strategy may be used to involve students in a group problem-solving activity in which they can benefit from communicating their own thinking and hearing other students' thinking.

How to use it:

1. Divide the class into collaborative groups, and provide each group with a word problem.

2. Explain to students that they are to solve this problem verbally. No writing or drawing may be done at any time during this step.

3. After the groups have discussed the problem and agreed how to solve it, members should take turns writing the steps to the solution in words rather than in mathematics symbols. Each group member must write one sentence and then pass the solution sheet to the next group member so he or she can add the next sentence.

4. After the groups have finished writing down all of the steps, ask each group to select one member to read the solution steps to the class while another writes the symbolic representation of this solution on the board.

5. Solicit volunteers from the other groups to write their version of this mathematics sentence on the board for the class to review.

Informational Text

Word Problem Roulette

Directions: Read each problem below, and discuss a solution with your group. Do not write anything during the discussion. This should be an oral discussion only. When the group is satisfied with the solution, write a group report of the solution, sentence by sentence. Each person in the group writes one sentence and then passes the solution report to another person to write the next sentence. Use only words (no symbols) to write the solution report.

1. A family of three adults and three children goes to an amusement park. Adult admission fare is twice as much as a child's. The family spends $81. How much is the adult admission fare?

2. A sale on swimsuits reduced the price on a two-piece suit from $45 to $27. What percent decrease does this represent?

Reflection Strategies

M-31. Learning Log

What is it?

An effective means of writing-to-learn is keeping a learning log. Learning logs can foster reflection on reading processes and hands-on activities to increase students' understanding. Learning logs differ from journals in that they focus on content covered in class, rather than on personal or private feelings. Students may reflect on how they feel, but it is always in relation to what is being studied in class. Santa and Havens (1991) suggest that teachers introduce learning logs to students as a way of writing down their thinking.

How could it be used in mathematics instruction?

Learning log entries may be incorporated across mathematics lessons. Writing activities can engage students in thinking about a concept and can help them examine more deeply the concept as they collect data or work with examples. Formulating explanations through writing helps students know if they really understand a concept. Writing can be used as a way to self-evaluate as students reflect on what they have learned.

How to use it:

1. Assign the topic. A learning log entry can be assigned at any time during class, depending upon the topic and your purpose.

2. Allow students "think time" to consider their response.

3. Give students time to write about the topic.

4. Encourage students to reread their learning log entries at a later date and reflect on how their ideas have changed.

For further discussion of this strategy, see the *TRCA Teacher's Manual*, pp. 148–150.

Reflection Strategies

Learning Log Assignment Example

The following are possible learning log topics, adapted from Brudnak (1998).

Before learning — to activate and assess prior knowledge

- Why do we use rulers (or scales or other measuring devices)?

- What do these symbols mean?

- Describe instances when you use addition at home.

- How is multiplication similar to addition?

- Make a web to describe some uses of fractions.

During learning — to help students identify how well they understand what is being covered in class

- Explain how you know that $7 + 3 = 11 - 1$.

- How do you know what a story problem is asking you to do?

- Write a story problem in which you need to calculate 5×7.

- Find examples in our classroom of the geometric shapes we are studying.

- Draw three pictures that demonstrate the concept of multiplication.

After the lesson — to help students reflect on their learning

- I have trouble understanding. . . .

- Write a note to a student who was absent from class and explain what was learned in class today about right triangles.

- Write a note to your parents explaining how you know when a shape has a line of symmetry.

- My favorite kind of story problem is. . . .

- Explain how you could do the calculation $65 - 19$ in your head.

M-32. Question-Answer Relationship (QAR)

What is it?

QAR (Raphael, 1982, 1986) is a strategy "designed to demystify the questioning process, providing teachers and students with a common vocabulary to discuss different types of questions and sources of information for answering these questions. . . " (Anthony & Raphael, 1996, p. 319). Four levels of questions are studied during strategy use and practice. Two are text-based QARs:

- "Right There" questions ask students to respond at the literal level; the words used to formulate and answer the questions can be found "right there" in the same sentence of the text.

- "Think and Search" questions require students to "think" about how the information or ideas in the text relate to one another, and to "search" through the entire passage they read to find information that applies.

The other QARs are knowledge based because students must use their prior knowledge to answer the question:

- "Author and You" questions require students to combine their prior knowledge with information gleaned from the text to answer the questions.

- "On My Own" questions can be answered with information from students' background knowledge; they do not require students to read the text.

How could it be used in mathematics instruction?

This strategy focuses on the relationship between questions and answers. It teaches students that answering different kinds of questions requires different reading behaviors and thought processes. That is, some questions require students to explore text to find an answer; some questions require students to explain something they have read; some questions require students to elaborate on what they have learned; and some questions ask students to evaluate their own thoughts about a topic.

How to use it:

1. Introduce the strategy by instructing students on each question-answer relationship.

2. Assign short passages to be read from the textbook. As students finish reading each passage, ask them one question from each QAR category. Point out the differences between each question and the kind of answer it requires.

3. After students demonstrate that they understand the differences among the four QAR levels, provide opportunities for students to practice identifying question-answer relationships.

4. Eventually, when reading is assigned in class, students should generate various QARs on their own that they present to the rest of the class for identification and answers.

For further discussion of this strategy, see the *TRCA Teacher's Manual*, pp. 145–147. For a discussion of a related strategy, concept question chain, see pp. 142–144 of the *TRCA Teacher's Manual*.

QAR Examples

Right There

- What is the additive identity?

- What is a distinguishing feature of a pentagon?

- What is the number that occurs most often in a set of data called?

- What is a name for a triangle with no congruent sides?

Reflection Strategies

Think and Search

- Explain the relationship between a rhombus and a parallelogram.

- What are the whole number solutions to $6 < x - 3 < 10$?

- What are three examples of numbers that are both square numbers and triangular numbers?

- Could a number be both a triangular number and a prime number?

Author and You

- Based on the author's description of a stem-and-leaf graph, identify some types of data that would be well represented in such a graph.

- For what data might it be useful to determine mean, mode, median, and range?

- What examples of tesselations have you seen in nature?

- Can you draw a shape that has exactly three lines of symmetry?

On My Own

- What might the number -5 represent in football?

- What types of graphs would you suggest the newspaper use to display information on sports scores?

- What kind (shape) of container would you recommend a company use to package candy?

- Describe an unusual use of numbers you have heard or seen in the newspaper.

Reflection Strategies

M-33. Questioning the Author (QtA)

What is it?

QtA (Beck, McKeown, Hamilton, & Kucan, 1998) is designed to assist students in their efforts to understand text as they read. The teacher selects a passage based on important concepts students will need to know and constructs queries, rather than traditional questions, to build understanding of concepts rather than simple recall of facts. Queries might include:

- What argument or point is the author trying to demonstrate here?

- What generalizations or conclusions is the author trying to make?

- What is the author describing or explaining?

Query-driven discussions create a community of learners grappling with an author's text and working together to understand it.

How could it be used in mathematics instruction?

Students are more likely to engage in reading difficult text if they know that they are part of a community of learners whose goal is to understand a topic. This strategy provides students with an opportunity to question their understanding of a topic as they read. It encourages them to explain their understanding of a topic to others. It allows them to elaborate and to make connections through discussions. It also allows them to evaluate what they may know and not know about a topic and to monitor and adjust their understanding based on the discussion.

How to use it:

1. Analyze and identify important concepts of a text, and decide how much of the text should be read at once. Decisions should be based on content, ideas, and information rather than on length of text.

Reflection Strategies

2. Develop queries or probes that will prompt discussion and build understanding.

3. Instruct students to read the selected passage.

4. Facilitate a query-driven discussion on a passage that requires students to grapple with ideas and to build understanding.

5. Provide time for students to understand this process by modeling how you might grapple with ideas to build understanding around a passage.

Examples of Queries

- What is the author saying about different ways of displaying data?

- What does the author mean by a "proportional relationship"?

- How does the author explain conditional probability?

- What is the author trying to say about the difference between categorical and numerical data?

- How does the author explain why "regular" is a property of polygons?

- What does the author mean by a "necessary and sufficient condition"?

- How did the author use examples to demonstrate the concept of random sampling?

- Why does the factor tree make sense given what the author told us about prime factorization?

- What is the author trying to say about the difference between rational numbers and decimal numbers?

- According to the author, what is the difference between dependent and independent events?

Reflection Strategies

Reflective

M-34. Role/Audience/Format/Topic (RAFT)

What is it?

The RAFT strategy (Santa, 1988) uses writing-to-learn activities to enhance understanding of informational text. Instead of writing a traditional essay explaining a concept learned, students demonstrate their understanding in a nontraditional format. This technique encourages creative thinking and motivates students to reflect in unusual ways about concepts they have read. RAFT is an acronym that stands for

- *Role of the writer*. What is the writer's role: reporter, observer, eyewitness?

- *Audience*. Who will be reading this writing: the teacher, other students, a parent, people in the community, an editor?

- *Format*. What is the best way to present this writing: in a letter, an article, a report, a poem?

- *Topic*. Who or what is the subject of this writing: a famous mathematician, an application of a procedure, a reaction to a specific event?

The RAFT strategy forces students to process information, rather than merely regurgitate factual answers to questions. Students are more motivated to undertake the writing assignment because it addresses various learning styles.

How could it be used in mathematics instruction?

This writing-to-learn strategy is an excellent way to involve students in explaining what they know about a mathematics topic and in further investigating the topic in a fun way.

How to use it:

1. Think about concepts or processes that you want students to learn from reading a selected passage. Consider how writing in a fun way may enhance students' understanding of the topic.

Reflection Strategies

2. Brainstorm possible roles students could assume in their writing.

3. Decide who the audience would be as well as the format for writing.

4. After students have finished reading, identify the role, audience, format, and topic (RAFT) for the writing. Assign the same role for all students, or let them choose from several different roles.

For further discussion of this strategy, see the *TRCA Teacher's Manual*, pp. 151–153.

RAFT Examples

Role	Audience	Format	Topic
Zero	Whole numbers	Campaign speech	Importance of the number 0
Scale factor	Architect	Directions for a blue print	Scale drawings
Percent	Student	Tip Sheet	Mental ways to calculate percents
Repeating decimal	Customers	Petition	Proof/check for set membership
Prime number	Rational numbers	Instructions	Rules for divisibility
Parts of a graph	TV audience	Script	How to read a graph
Exponent	Jury	Instructions to the jury	Laws of exponents
One	Whole numbers	Advice column	Perfect, abundant, deficient, amicable numbers
Variable	Equations	Letter	Role of variables
Container	Self	Diary	Comparing volume measurements
Acute triangle	Obtuse triangle	Letter	Explain differences of triangles
Function	Relations	Article	Argue the importance of functions

Note: Basic format only from *Classroom Strategies for Interactive Learning, Second Edition* by D. Buehl, 2001, Newark, DE: International Reading Association. Copyright 2001 by the International Reading Association.

Reflection Strategies

M-35. Writing to Learn

What is it?

Writing to learn is a method "that can (and should) be incorporated across the curriculum. This approach helps students personalize learning so that they understand their course work better and retain what they have learned longer. It also encourages high-level thinking skills" (Sebranek, Meyer, & Kemper, 1996, p. 44). Writing-to-learn activities can be used to help students reflect on and explore ideas and concepts they are reading about in class, thereby helping students to construct meaning. As with learning log entries, these writing activities are intended to be brief and can be assigned at any point during the class period.

How could it be used in mathematics instruction?

Writing activities can engage students in thinking and reasoning about a concept. When students communicate their understanding of a concept in writing, they confront what they know and need to learn about this concept, that is, how well they understand the concept. Writing may be used as a way for students to reflect on what they have learned.

How to use it:

1. Select the concept you want students to explore.

2. Assign the writing-to-learn activity at any time during class, depending upon the topic and your purpose. The suggestions below are grouped into prereading, during reading, and after reading activities. When designing a writing topic, remember that the task should not require students merely to regurgitate facts from the text. Instead, it should ask students to reflect on or apply what they are learning.

3. Assign the topic, and give students three to five minutes "think time" to consider their response.

Reflection Strategies

4. Allow about five minutes for students to write on the topic. Remind them that you will be assessing their responses based on the depth of thought evident in their writing.

Prereading

- **Alphabet Soup.** This activity can be used to activate students' prior knowledge. On the first day of a unit, students work in groups to complete the pre-reading sections of a K-W-L worksheet (see page 110) or pre-reading plan (see page 115). After group collaboration, students spend five minutes individually writing about their prior knowledge. If the topic is new to most students, explain it in brief terms and suggest students write for five minutes about any impressions they have about the subject.

- **Anticipation Guides.** Students complete a true-false anticipation guide on the subject of the unit. Before they discuss their answers as a class, students select one or two of the guide's statements and write for five minutes, defending their answer for that statement.

- **Problematic Situations.** Instead of discussing as a group potential solutions to a problematic situation, students write their own solutions to the problem.

- **Yesterday's News.** Students spend five minutes at the beginning of class writing a note to a student (real or fictional) who missed the previous class. In their notes, students explain how one idea from that class (they select which concept or point to discuss) is particularly important.

- **One-liners.** At the beginning of class, students write one sentence about the importance or relevance of something they learned in the previous lesson.

Reflection Strategies

During Class/Reading

- **Fast Food for Thought.** After explaining a particular concept, process, or vocabulary term, direct students to write a question they still have about the topic. Ask students to exchange papers and either answer the writer's question or suggest resources they could use to locate the answer.

- **Out of This World.** At a convenient point during a lesson, allow 10 minutes for students to write about the following: You are an alien from another galaxy. Your spacecraft just landed outside of the school building and your first stop is in our classroom. Write your observations of the lesson, the teacher, and the students in the class.

After the Lesson/Reading

- **Dear Diary.** Ask students to assume the identity of an historic figure who is/was intimately involved in the lesson topic and to write a diary entry as if they were that individual. For example, students studying Fibonacci numbers might assume the role of Fibonacci and compose a diary entry chronicling his thoughts on the sequence of numbers.

- **Read the Instructions.** Students write instructions for how to solve a problem or perform a skill they have just learned.

- **The Last Word.** Students spend the last 10 minutes of class writing you a letter about something they do not understand or need help with in the current unit. In addition to revealing to students what they do not know, this writing task can inform you about what needs to be reviewed or clarified during the next lesson.

Reflection Strategies

- **"And the Winner Is . . . . "** This activity works best at the end of a unit as it is a student-led form of review. Let students brainstorm on the following: The publisher of the textbook we use wants students' input on the content of the unit we are studying. Specifically, they want to know which section or concept included in this unit has been most interesting and why. Once students consider possibilities collectively, let each student write a letter to the publisher identifying his or her choice and citing specific reasons for the nomination.

For further discussion of this strategy, see the *TRCA Teacher's Manual*, pp. 154–157.

MCREL

Bibliography

Anthony, H. M., & Raphael, T. E. (1996). Using questioning strategies to promote students' active comprehension of content area material. In D. Lapp, J. Flood, & Farnan (Eds.), *Content area reading and learning: Instructional strategies* (pp. 307–322). Needham Heights, MA: Allyn & Bacon.

Armbruster, B. B. (1996). Considerate texts. In D. Lapp, J. Flood, & N. Farnan (Eds.), *Content area reading and learning: Instructional strategies* (pp. 47–57). Needham Heights, MA: Allyn & Bacon.

Baldwin, R. S., Ford, J. C., & Readence, J. E. (1981). Teaching word connotations: An alternative strategy. *Reading World, 21*, 103–108.

Beck, I. L., McKeown, M. G., Hamilton, R. L., & Kucan, L. (1998, Spring/Summer). Getting at the meaning: How to help students unpack difficult text. *American Educator, 85*, 66–71.

Borasi, R., Siegel, M., Fonzi, J., & Smith, C. F. (1998). Using transactional reading strategies to support sense-making and discussion in mathematics classrooms: An exploratory study. *Journal for Research in Mathematics Education, 29*(3), 275–305.

Billstein, R., & Williamson, J. (1999). *Math thematics* (Book 2). Evanston, IL: McDougal Littell.

Braselton, S., & Decker, B. C. (1994, November). Using graphic organizers to improve the reading of mathematics. *The Reading Teacher, 48*(3), 276–281.

Brennan, A. D., & Dunlap, W. P. (1985). What are the prime factors of reading mathematics? *Reading Improvement, 22*, 152–159.

Brown, A. L., Day, J. D., & Jones, R. (1983). The development of plans for summarizing texts. *Child Development, 54*, 968–979.

Brudnak, K. A. (1998, January/February). What works in math: Math communication. *Learning, 26*(4), 38–49.

Buehl, D. (1995). Classroom strategies for interactive learning. *Monograph of the Wisconsin State Reading Association*. Scholfield, WI: Wisconsin State Reading Association.

Burton, G. M., Hopkins, M. H., Johnson, H. C., Kaplan, J. D., Kennedy, L., & Schultz, K.A. (1994). *Mathematics plus*. Orlando, FL: Harcourt Brace.

Costa, A. L., & Garmston, R. J. (1994). *Cognitive coaching: A foundation for renaissance schools*. Norwood, MA: Christopher-Gordon.

Bibliography

Culyer, R. C. (1988). Reading and mathematics go hand in hand. *Reading Improvement, 25*, 189–195.

Davey, B. (1983). Think aloud: Modeling the cognitive processes of reading comprehension. *Journal of Reading, 27*(1), 44–47.

Davis, S. J., & Gerber, R. (1994, September). Open to suggestion: Content area strategies in secondary mathematics classrooms. *Journal of Reading, 38*(1), 55–57.

Dickson, S. V., Simmons, D. C., & Kameenni, E. J. (1995, February). *Text organization and its relation to reading comprehension: A synthesis of the research* (Technical Report No. 17). Eugene, OR: National Center to Improve the Tools of Educators, University of Oregon.

Dickson, S. V., Simmons, D. C., & Kameenui, E. J. (1995). *Text organization: Curricular and instructional implications for diverse learners* (Technical Report No. 19). Eugene, OR: National Center to Improve the Tools of Educators, University of Oregon.

Earle, R. (1976). *Teaching reading and mathematics*. Newark, DE: International Reading Association.

Earp, N. W. (1970, April). Observations on teaching reading in mathematics. *Journal of Reading, 13*, 529–33.

Earp, N. W., & Tanner, F. W. (1980, December). Mathematics and language. *Arithmetic Teacher, 28*(4), 32–34.

Fay, L. (1965). Reading study skills: Math and science. In J. A. Figural (Ed.), *Reading and Inquiry* (pp. 93–94). Newark, DE: International Reading Association.

Fraenkel, J. R. (1973). *Helping students think and value: Strategies for teaching the social studies*. Englewood Cliffs, NJ: Prentice-Hall.

Frayer, D. A., Frederick, W. C., & Klausmeier, H. J. (1969). *A schema for testing the level of concept mastery* (Technical Report No. 16). Madison, WI: University of Wisconsin, Research and Development Center for Cognitive Learning.

Fuentes, P. (1998, November/December). Reading comprehension in mathematics. *The Clearing House, 72*(2), 81–88.

Gay, A. S. (1999, September). Is problem solving in middle school mathematics "normal"? *Middle School Journal, 31*(1), 41–47.

Gillett, J. W., & Temple, C. (1983). *Understanding reading problems: Assessment and instruction*. Boston: Little, Brown.

McREL

Bibliography

Harste, J., & Short, K. (with Burke, C.). (1988). *Creating classrooms for authors*. Portsmouth, NH: Heinemann.

Helwig, R., Rozek-Tedesco, M., Tindal, G., Heath, B., & Almond, P. (1999, December). Reading as an access to mathematics problem solving on multiple-choice tests for sixth-grade students. *Journal of Educational Research, 93*(2), 113–125.

Herber, H. (1978). *Teaching reading in content areas* (2nd ed.). Englewood Cliffs, NJ: Prentice Hall.

Holloway, J. H. (1999, October). Improving the reading skills of adolescents. *Educational Leadership, 57*(2), 80–81.

Johnson, D. D., & Pearson, P. D. (1984). *Teaching reading vocabulary* (2nd ed.). New York: Holt, Rinehart & Winston.

Jones, B. F., Palincsar, A. S., Ogle, D. S. & Carr, E. G. (Eds.). (1987). *Strategic teaching and learning: Cognitive instruction in the content areas*. Alexandria, VA and Elmhurst, IL: Association for Supervision and Curriculum Development and North Central Regional Educational Laboratory.

Kresse, E. C. (1984, April). Using reading as a thinking process to solve mathematics story problems. *Journal of Reading, 27*, 598–601.

Langer, L. A. (1981, November). From theory to practice: A prereading plan. *Journal of Reading, 25*, 152–156.

Lindquist, M. M. (1987). Strategic teaching in mathematics. In B. F. Jones, A. S. Palincsar, D. S. Ogle, & E. G. Carr (Eds.), *Strategic teaching and learning: Cognitive instruction in the content areas* (pp. 111–134). Alexandria, VA and Elmhurst, IL: Association for Supervision and Curriculum Development and the North Central Regional Educational Laboratory.

Martinez, J. G. R., & Martinez, N. C. (2001). *Reading and writing to learn mathematics: A guide and a resource book*. Boston: Allyn & Bacon.

Marzano, R. J., Pickering, D. J., & Pollock J. E. (2001). *Classroom instruction that works: Research-based strategies for increasing student achievement*. Alexandria, VA: Association for Supervision and Curriculum Development.

Monroe, E. E. (1997). *Using graphic organizers to teach vocabulary: How does available research inform mathematics instruction?* (ERIC Document Reproduction Service No. ED 414 256)

Bibliography

Monroe, E. E., & Pendergrass, M. R. (1997). *Effects of mathematical vocabulary instruction on fourth grade students.* Paper presented at the 1997 Brigham Young University Public School Partnership Symposium on Education. (ERIC Document Reproduction Service No. ED 414 182)

Murdock, J., Kamischke, E., & Kamischke, E. (2000). *Discovering algebra: An investigative approach* (Preliminary Ed. Vol. 1). Emeryville, CA: Key Curriculum Press.

Musthafa, B. (1996). *Learning from texts and reading instruction.* (ERIC Document Reproduction Service No. ED 395 268)

National Council of Teachers of Mathematics. (1989). *Curriculum and evaluation standards for school mathematics.* Reston, VA: Author.

National Council of Teachers of Mathematics. (1991). *Professional standards for teaching mathematics.* Reston, VA: Author.

National Council of Teachers of Mathematics. (2000). *Principles and standards for school mathematics.* Reston, VA: Author.

National Research Council, Mathematical Sciences Education Board. (1989). *Everybody counts: A report to the nation on the future of mathematics education.* Washington, DC: National Academy Press.

National Research Council, Mathematical Sciences Education Board. (1990). *Reshaping school mathematics: A philosophy and framework for curriculum.* Washington, DC: National Academy Press.

Ogle, D. (1986, February). The K-W-L: A teaching model that develops active reading of expository text. *The Reading Teacher, 39,* 564–570.

Ogle, D. (1989). The know, want to know, learning strategy. In K. D. Muth (Ed.), *Children's comprehension of text* (pp. 205–223). Newark, DE: International Reading Association.

Olson, M. W., & Gee, T. C. (1991). Content reading instruction in the primary grades: Perceptions and strategies. *The Reading Teacher, 45*(4), 298–306.

Palincsar, A. S., & Brown, A. L. (1985). Reciprocal teaching: Activities to promote "reading with your mind." In T. L. Harris & E. J. Cooper (Eds.), *Reading, thinking, and concept development* (pp. 147–158). New York: College Board Publications.

Papy, F. (1986). *A valentine mystery.* Aurora, CO: Mid-continent Research for Education and Learning.

McREL

Bibliography

Polya, G. (1957). *How to solve it: A new aspect of mathematical method* (2nd ed.). Princeton, NJ: Princeton University Press.

Raphael, T. E. (1982). Question-answering strategies for children. *The Reading Teacher, 36,* 186–190.

Raphael, T. E. (1986). Teaching question-answer relationships, revisited. *The Reading Teacher, 39,* 516–522.

Readence, J. E., Bean, T. W., & Baldwin, R. S. (2001). *Content area literacy: An integrated approach* (7th ed.). Dubuque, IA: Kendall Hunt.

Reehm, S. P. & Long, S. A. (1996, May). Reading in the mathematics classroom. *Middle School Journal, 27*(5), 35–41.

Reutzel, D. R. (1983, October). C^6: A reading model for teaching arithmetic story problem solving. *The Reading Teacher, 37,* 28–35.

Robinson, F. (1961). *Effective study.* New York: Harper & Row.

Roe, B., Stoodt, B., & Burns, P. C. (1995). *Secondary school literacy instruction: The content areas* (5th ed.). Boston: Houghton Mifflin.

Santa, C. M. (1988). *Content reading including study systems.* Dubuque, IA: Kendall-Hunt.

Santa, C. M., & Havens, L. T. (1991). Learning through writing. In C. M. Santa & D. E. Alverman (Eds.), *Science learning: Processes and applications* (pp. 122–133). Newark, DE: International Reading Association.

Schwartz, R. (1988, November). Learning to learn vocabulary in content area textbooks. *Journal of Reading, 32,* 108–117.

Sebranek, P., Meyer, V., & Kemper, D. (1996). *A teacher's guide to accompany Writers Inc.* Wilmington, MA: Write Source.

Shuard, H., & Rothery, A. (Eds.). (1984). *Children reading mathematics.* Athenaeum Press: Newcastle upon Tyne, England.

Siegel, M., & Borasia, R. (1992). Toward a new integration of reading in mathematics instruction. *Focus on Learning Problems in Mathematics, 14*(2), 18–36.

Smith, C. F., & Kepner, H. S., Jr. (with Kane, R. B.). (1981). *Reading in the mathematics classroom.* Washington, DC: National Education Association.

Bibliography

Stahl, S. A., & Fairbanks, M. M. (1986, Spring). The effects of vocabulary instruction: A model-based meta-analysis. *Review of Education Research, 56*(1), 72–110.

Taba, H., Durkin, M. C., Fraenkel, J. R., & McNaughton, A. (1971). *A teacher's handbook to elementary social studies: An inductive approach.* Reading, MA: Addison-Wesley.

Thomas, D. A. (1988). Reading and reasoning skills for mathematics problem solvers. *Journal of Reading, 32,* 244–249.

Vacca, R. T., & Vacca, J. L. (1993). *Content area reading* (4th ed.). New York: HarperCollins.

Vacca, R. T., & Vacca, J. L. (1999). *Content area reading: Literacy and learning across the curriculum* (6th ed.). Menlo Park, CA: Longman.

Wisconsin Center for Education Research. (n.d.). *Mathematics for parents: Newsletter on place value.* Madison, WI: Author. Retrieved December 29, 2001, from http://www.wcer.wisc.edu/MIMS/ParentNewsletters/Place_Value/newsletter14.html

McREL

About the Authors

Mary Lee Barton, M.S. Ed., has worked in the areas of literacy, learning, and professional development for more than 25 years. She brings a wealth of practical classroom experience to her writing and professional development workshops. As a consultant for McREL, Barton coauthored *Teaching Reading in the Content Areas: If Not Me, Then Who?* and its supplements, *Teaching Reading in Mathematics, Teaching Reading in Science*, and *Teaching Reading in Social Studies*. Her articles "Addressing the Literacy Crisis: Teaching Reading in the Content Areas" and "Motivating Students to Read Their Textbooks" have appeared in the NASSP Bulletin. She has trained thousands of teachers and administrators across the country in content- area reading and writing instruction. Currently, Barton is a writer and a business and education consultant in private practice. She trains and provides technical assistance nationally to educators and business clients on literacy issues in education and in the workplace.

Clare Heidema worked for many years with the educational laboratories CEMREL and McREL, focusing on curriculum development, professional development, dissemination, and product development in mathematics education. She was principal author of the *Comprehensive School Mathematics Program* (CSMP) and served as director of the CSMP Developer/Demonstrator project for the National Diffusion Network from 1983 – 1996. She also served as a mathematics consultant for the Eisenhower Regional Consortium at McREL. Heidema is a former middle and high school mathematics teacher and has had teaching experience at all levels from elementary school to graduate school. She holds a BA/MA in mathematics, teaching certification from the University of Michigan, and has completed MS and doctoral requirements (ABD) in mathematics from Syracuse University. She has presented at numerous state, regional, and national conferences. Heidema currently works as an educational consultant.

Teaching Reading in Mathematics

TRAINING WORKSHOPS AVAILABLE

McREL delivers training and consultation on its series, *Teaching Reading in the Content Areas: If Not Me, Then Who?*, *Teaching Reading in Mathematics*, *Teaching Reading in Science*, and *Teaching Reading in Social Studies* to teachers, reading specialists, staff developers, and administrators.

These workshops focus on a framework for teaching reading in the content areas, and provide numerous strategies to help students better comprehend content-area reading material. Strategies emphasize students monitoring their own thinking, selecting appropriate strategies, and applying these strategies to increase their awareness and understanding of text.

The **Teacher Workshop** (designed for 4–12 educators) provides an overview of content-area reading instruction; engages participants in applying vocabulary, reading, and reflection strategies to specific content covered in their classrooms; and offers practical suggestions on integrating these strategies into existing curricula.

For more information about scheduling workshops and consulting services, contact **McREL** at **303-337-0990**, or visit our website at **www.mcrel.org**.

McREL